moving from
judgment

moving from

judgment

how to have an open
heart in a closed world

joseph & brenda rinehart

TATE PUBLISHING *& Enterprises*

Scripture quotations marked (TNIV) are taken from the *Holy Bible, Today's New International Version*, copyright © 2001, 2005 by Biblica, Inc.™ Used by permission of Zondervan. All rights reserved worldwide. www.zondervan.com.

Scripture quotations marked "NIV" are taken from the *Holy Bible, New International Version ®*, Copyright © 1973, 1978, 1984 by International Bible Society. Used by permission of Zondervan Publishing House. All rights reserved.

This book is designed to provide accurate and authoritative information with regard to the subject matter covered. This information is given with the understanding that neither the author nor Tate Publishing, LLC is engaged in rendering legal, professional advice. Since the details of your situation are fact dependent, you should additionally seek the services of a competent professional..

The opinions expressed by the author are not necessarily those of Tate Publishing, LLC.

Published by Tate Publishing & Enterprises, LLC
127 E. Trade Center Terrace | Mustang, Oklahoma 73064 USA
1.888.361.9473 | www.tatepublishing.com

Tate Publishing is committed to excellence in the publishing industry. The company reflects the philosophy established by the founders, based on Psalm 68:11,
"The Lord gave the word and great was the company of those who published it."

Book design copyright © 2011 by Tate Publishing, LLC. All rights reserved.
Cover design by Anna Lee
Interior design by Sarah Kirchen
Illustration by

Published in the United States of America

ISBN: 978-1-61777-620-5
1. Religion / Christian Life / Social Issues
2. Religion / Christian Life / General
11.05.10

We dedicate this book, first to the LORD Jesus Christ, the very center of our lives and reason for being.

Second, to Brooklake Community Church and our Bible study group for inspiring us to write it, and finally, to our family who continually motivates us!

Table of Contents

Preface 11

Red Light, Green Light. 15

King of the Hill: Framing the Issues 21

   Going Deeper 26

   Questions 36

   Prayer. 37

Hide and Seek: Personhood. 39

   Going Deeper 51

   Questions 61

   Prayer. 62

Duck, Duck, Goose: Personal Values 63

   Family 67

   Personal Experience 68

   Popular Culture 69

   Preferences 69

Nature 70

Going Deeper 75

Questions 85

General Values Key 86

Prayer 88

Red Rover, Red Rover: Cultural Values 89

Historical Cultural Group: The Jews 93

Modern Corollary: Churched Christians 94

Historical Cultural Group: The Gentiles 96

Modern Corollary: The Unchurched
and/or Non-Religious 98

Historical Cultural Group: The Samaritans 99

Modern Corollary: The Once-Churched 101

Going Deeper 105

Questions 116

Prayer 117

Truth or Dare: Acceptance 119

Going Deeper 132

Questions 144

Prayer 145

Tug of War: Moving Past Judgment 147

Acknowledge the Hurt 152

Give Yourself Time 153

Don't Pick at Your Scabs .154

Let the Train Leave the Station. 156

Understand the Nature of Cause and Effect. 159

Use Your Hurt to Heal Others 161

Going Deeper 163

Questions 172

Prayer. 173

Capture the Flag: Putting It All Together 175

Going Deeper 183

Questions 198

Prayer. 199

End Notes. 201

Bibliography 207

Preface

Ever marvel at the way Jesus interacted with the woman at the well, the prostitute who poured the fine perfume on Jesus's feet in preparation for his burial, the woman caught in adultery that was about to be stoned, or the tax collector, Zaccheus? Jesus at no time condoned the actions of the individuals, but meeting Jesus completely transformed their lives; just getting to know Him seemed to reach them at the deepest level and empowered them to turn away from their sin.

In some instances, the interactions were brief, yet very powerful. The interactions were not focused on the sin of the individual but on love and forgiveness. Even when Jesus could have focused on the politics of the day, he chose very purposefully to focus on the worth of the individual.

This book is intended for personal study—one way to examine our hearts and ask, "Are we looking at others with the eyes of Christ?" It is so easy to judge another person's motives, in essence to judge their heart, without ever considering their journey.

If we are honest, all of us would admit to having some type of personal bias and sometimes, whether we intend to or not, that bias turns to judgment. Even as my husband and I write this book we have had to rewrite sections of it to avoid sounding judgmental, which is the very thing we are trying not to be.

In essence, that very plight is what led us to write the book in the first place. For example, we have a heart for the homeless and support that type of ministry in addition to others. It's very easy for us to look at a homeless person standing on the street corner and offer them something to eat. It does not matter to us what the person did to get to there, it does not matter if he or she could work, and it does not matter if he or she is thankful.

We do not spend one single moment examining any of these things. We give what we have out of love and because we believe that Christ has called us to do it. On the other hand, let someone cut us off in traffic, and that might be a completely different story.

What about the severely overweight person in the motorized wheelchair that just ordered two burgers, fries, and a shake at the counter in front of us? What about the person collecting social security disability that goes fishing every weekend while we head off to work our second or third job? What do we think about them?

It doesn't have to make sense because the simple truth is that no matter how much we want to do the right thing and see other's through Jesus's eyes, we are flawed human beings, and we mess up—a lot.

My husband and I have backgrounds in ministry in various capacities, and most recently led a study group together in our home for two years. As we developed the material for this book, we used it as study material for the group, building lessons out of each chapter.

As a result, the chapters are divided into three sections: basic text designed for understanding the concepts discussed, a going deeper section for personal or group study, and a prayer section that is specific to the material covered in the chapter.

When we decided to write this book, our intention was to help ourselves as well as the reader. We wrote it based on our personal experiences in life, in ministry, at our jobs, and with our many children. The titles of the chapters—games we played as children—were developed out of a simple question posed to our children, "Name a game you played as a child that made you feel included." In concert, they replied, "All of them." It is our prayer that the reader will feel included and find a nugget or two of inspiration and wisdom in the text.

— *Brenda*

Red Light, Green Light

The best time to play Red Light, Green Light was on a summer night when all the kids in the neighborhood would be playing in the courtyard after dinner. It was such a pleasure to be the "one" with all the power; the one pressed up against the wooden fence hollering out the orders of red light and green light—eyes keenly inspecting the other children for violations of movement post the red light command.

In reality, the "one" didn't have any real power at all because any violation of movement was then voted on by the other children.

"He did not move."

"Yes, he did!"

"Did I, did I move?" and so on until a consensus was formed and the accused withdrew or stayed put…

— *Brenda*

"Are we taking in just anybody?"

The stern voice at the other end of the phone belonged to Miriam (name changed to provide anonymity), who served as the project manager and treasurer for the new church I had been called to help establish just north of Memphis, Tennessee.

"Excuse me?" I asked, honestly having no earthly clue what she was getting at.

"Are we taking in just anybody? We certainly can't accept Assembly of God folks and not those Independent Baptists because they think they're predestined!" Miriam complained in her syrupy accent. "They will simply *have* to be re-baptized!"

I remember being nearly speechless at the idea that almost every person attending the new congregation would essentially have to have their IDs checked before joining the church, helping with the offering, or singing in the choir—that sounded more like the exclusivity of a country club or the filtering of minors from entering a drinking establishment than what would go on in a church.

In reality, it was not a real question; it was a warning—a warning that the self-elected power brokers had a radically different agenda for that developing congregation than I did. *My* understanding of Christianity viewed the so-called "outsiders" as the whole point of "doing church" to begin with, not treating them as modern lepers.

However, as most young idealists do, I chose to ignore that warning with the assurance that God was on my side, and that right would indeed prevail, a notion that suffered badly when I found myself forced out a short eighteen months or so later.

The reasons can be summed up as "letting the wrong kind of people in," "not being Baptist enough," or "being a novice," as the accusations were essentially phrased. In retrospect, however, the behaviors and attitudes that created that "in-crowd" mindset have permeated Christianity for a substantial period of time and are often lampooned by stand-up comedians, movies, and popular late-night television shows such as *Saturday Night Live.*

In fact, one of the most famous caricatures of this exclusivist view of Christianity is framed with the words, "Well isn't *that* special?"—the immortal question asked by Dana Carvey's character, the "Church Lady." Carvey's satirical portrayal of the 1950s style woman is positively brilliant—the horn-rimmed glasses, print dress, uptight demeanor, and complete with more catchphrases than a modern-day superhero!

The "Church Lady" was amazingly funny and wildly entertaining because it reflected reality and common experience regardless of religion, denomination, or geography. Unfortunately, the actuality reflected in "Church Chat" is anything but comical, and younger generations seem well attuned to that.

Changing our self-centered nature requires more than just claiming a genuine religious/spiritual experience, making resolutions regarding our attitudes, or attending a self-help seminar. Genuine transformation occurs as a journey and usually takes a lifetime.

This book will focus on some of the core issues of judgment, which can help each of us to perform honest self-appraisals, and then take steps to make changes. Of course, starting on a trip with no sense of direction or guide-map can result in "scenic detours" that seldom result in an enjoyable experience.

When I moved my family to Washington State from Tennessee, we drove near Yellowstone National Park and decided to take "Beartooth Pass" to view the area. What looked like a short road actually turned out to be a long, two-lane, winding road along cliffs and sheer drops, jammed with tons of vehicles.

Suffice it to say that while several routes may exist for a specific destination, usually one is more optimal than the rest. With that in mind, please consider the rest of the material in this book as a navigational chart. The following is an outline of the journey:

1. King of the Hill: Framing the Issues - "Starting the Discussion"

2. Hide and Seek: Personhood—"What it means to be a person/human being"

3. Duck, Duck, Goose: Personal Values—"What we choose to value, prioritize, and live by"

4. Red Rover, Red Rover: Cultural Values—"Societal values that we choose to accept and live by"

5. Truth or Dare: Acceptance–"Personal arrogance with regard to personal values and/or culture: MY values are better than YOUR values"

6. Tug of War: Moving Past Judgment–"Getting past experiences when others have passed judgment on you"

7. Capture the Flag: Putting It all Together–"Balancing the scales of values"

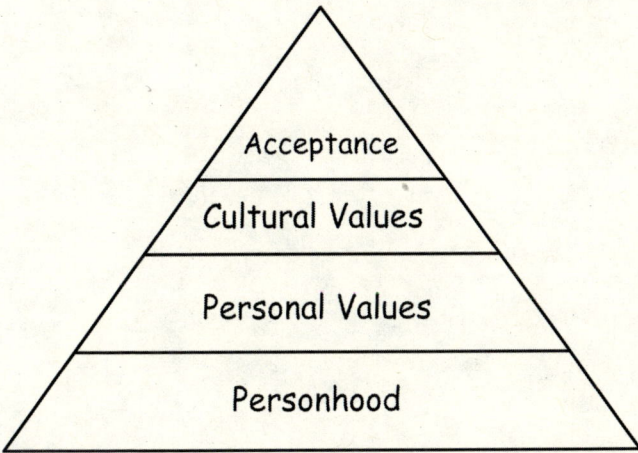

As you can see, each section builds upon the other, resulting in a better grasp of the whole business of relating to others in the world in which we find ourselves. Each chapter will deal with a separate topic using various references and thoughts that you should find easy to read and enjoyable.

Some of the material is designed to create more questions than answers, other pieces may simply provoke a reaction, and some pieces may just create an opportunity for self-evaluation. At the end of each chapter you will find a "Going Deeper" section, giving you the opportunity to dig well below the surface and explore issues in much greater detail.

Following the Going Deeper section will be a list of "Questions" to stimulate additional thought. The final section of each chapter focuses on "Prayer," asking Jesus to reveal Himself through the entire process.

King of the Hill: Framing the Issues

If you judge people, you have no time to love them.

Mother Teresa

King of the Hill was a dangerous game. At least that's what my mother said. It was akin to the fight for dominance expressed by most "alpha" males in a pack of animals. In fact, I often visualized two rams at the top of the mountain butting horns until one ultimately fell to his death on the jagged rocks below.

Of course, I was seven, so the ram that fell never actually died, but the picture is pretty much the same. Funny thing though, when you're a child there is a direct correlation to how much you like something and how much your mother doesn't—until you get hurt...

—*Brenda*

Probably one of the greatest principles I have learned in my adult life is summarized by the well-known phrase—perception is reality! Philosophers argue about the nature of truth, scientists accept only provable truth, and religious teachers declare spiritual or eternal truth.

While truth is indeed important, from a relationship standpoint, how others perceive us often carries more weight than what we believe or what we say. About ten years ago, I was one of two sales engineers supporting a three-state region in the Pacific Northwest and learned very quickly that if I was not physically in the office that it could easily be assumed that I was not working at all.

The truth was that I was assisting a group of about a dozen account executives that required a lot of activity and hard work. The truth in this case was irrelevant, because the perception was "out of sight, out on the golf course" or something similar. To dispel that myth required effort, lots of regular communication, status reports, and getting work done on or before deadlines.

In my professional life I would have committed career suicide by ignoring the importance of managing perception. Christianity in modern times faces the same kind of issue regarding perception. From local gossip to national headlines, scandals regarding church leaders and members of all denominations are too prevalent.

In the court of public opinion, Christians have been cast in a less than favorable light by many in the U.S. David Kinnaman, president of the Barna Research Group, conducted a 2007 survey to understand the opinions of Christianity to young people between the ages of sixteen to twenty-nine. According to this research, non-Christians in this age bracket had the following perceptions:

Christianity is Anti-Gay	91 percent
Christianity is Judgmental	87 percent
Christianity is Hypocritical	85 percent[1]

While this survey specifically measures young people, one can reasonably infer similar attitudes among other age groups as well, which can be supported by numerous anecdotal experiences, some of which I have personally heard or experienced over the years.

Imagine if you will, walking out of a local family restaurant to encounter a pickup truck at the edge of the parking lot with posters (pictured below) depicting the very viewpoint described by Kinnaman.

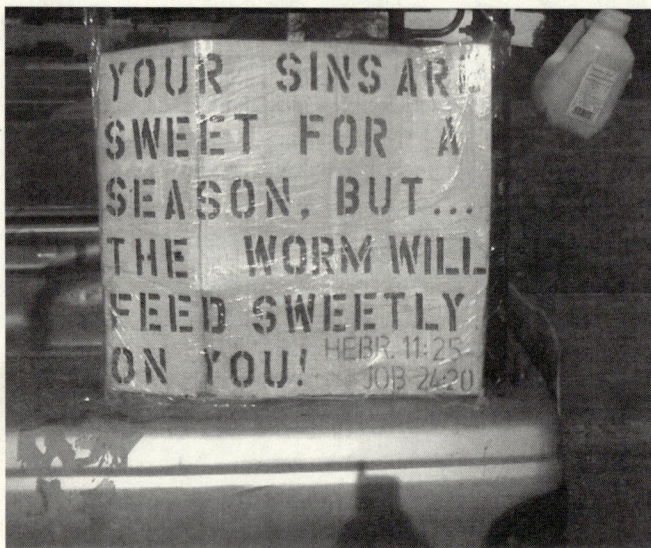

YOUR SINS ARE SWEET FOR A SEASON, BUT... THE WORM WILL FEED SWEETLY ON YOU! HEBR. 11:25 JOB 24:20

Unfortunately, this phenomenon is neither recent nor new, as evidenced by Jesus's own violent clash with the religious establishment of His own day, which culminated in His own death at the hands of the Romans.

Studying the viewpoints of these opposing forces is rather revealing; their vehemence had as much to do with the content of the teachings of Jesus as with the company He kept.

Jesus of Nazareth was radically different than any other religious leader or teacher of His day, not merely because of His claims to deity, but in how He approached people and the way they responded to Him. The various sectarian groups of Judaism at the time practiced a sort of religious elitism, creating spiritual castes of those worthy and those less than worthy.

Jesus took the exact opposite approach and essentially turned the hierarchy upside down, and the "common sinners" of that time flocked to Him with a powerful magnetism. This raises the obvious question of how a spiritual movement based on love, acceptance, and the inclusion of "outsiders" morphed into the kind of stereotype pictured by "the Church Lady."

The short answer is due to a pervasive attitude of *judgment*.

I can hear the resounding "yes" from many quarters of society, at a pitch so loud and intense that it would probably shatter glass, in the same way an opera singer would disintegrate a goblet. The inherent hypocrisy in that, however, is that modern expressions of Christian churches are not alone in that collective "sin."

If you peel back the layers a bit, proverbially speaking, you can hear similar venom from an entire chorus of different social groups, each with their own agendas and whose words and attitudes are strikingly similar. Truth be told, if we try to take an honest and objective look at ourselves, the simple fact is that as human beings we *all* have the tendency to pass judgment on one another.

That can manifest itself as a superiority complex—"I am better than you"—although it often sounds like the more sinister and subtle arrogance of "I can do better," "I am right," "I am the boss," or similar expressions. This is in direct contrast with the words of Jesus when He said, "First remove the log from your own eye."

Remember high school? Teenagers hand out judgment like it's candy, valuing people by the label on their clothes, the cars they drive, the people they hang out with, their level of popularity, and so on and so forth. Come to think of it, certain segments of adult society do that as well, the ones that shop at Walmart look down their nose at those that shop at Nordstrom's or Sak's, and vice-versa—I guess it shows that we are all *equal opportunity offenders*!

The universal problem of humanity centers on the fact that we view the world with ourselves at the center, rather than God. Sometimes the reactions come out of insecurity (we feel threatened), so we find a way to reduce someone else to our level by classifying them as inferior in some form or fashion.

At other times it may spring out of some experience in our past, in which we are reacting to someone else and projecting it on the person we may be dealing with. Other causes can range from simple ignorance, fear of the unknown, repressed anger, sheer arrogance, etc.

Going Deeper

The LORD said to Samuel, "How long will you mourn for Saul, since I have rejected him as king over Israel? Fill your horn with oil and be on your way; I am sending you to Jesse of Bethlehem. I have chosen one of his sons to be king."

But Samuel said, "How can I go? Saul will hear about it and kill me." The LORD said, "Take a heifer with you and say, 'I have come to sacrifice to the LORD.' Invite Jesse to the sacrifice, and I will show you what to do. You are to anoint for me the one I indicate."

Samuel did what the LORD said. When he arrived at Bethlehem, the elders of the town trembled when they met him. They asked, "Do you come in peace?" Samuel replied, "Yes, in peace; I have come to sacrifice to the LORD. Consecrate yourselves and come to the sacrifice with me." Then he consecrated Jesse and his sons and invited them to the sacrifice. When they arrived, Samuel saw Eliab and thought, "Surely the LORD's anointed stands here before the LORD." But the LORD said to Samuel, "Do not consider his appearance or his height, for I have rejected him.

The LORD does not look at the things man looks at. Man looks at the outward appearance, but the LORD looks at the heart."... Jesse had seven of his sons pass before Samuel, but Samuel said to him, "The LORD has not chosen these." So he asked Jesse, "Are these all the sons you have?" "There is still the youngest," Jesse answered, "but he is tending the sheep." Samuel said, "Send for him; we will not sit down until he arrives." So he sent and had him brought in. He was ruddy, with a fine appearance and handsome features. Then the LORD said, "Rise and anoint him; he is the one."

1 Samuel 16:1–12 (NIV)

Background:

Israel inaugurated its monarchy during the lifetime of the prophet Samuel in approximately the year 1050 b.c. when the people clamored for a king. Samuel had warned them that this was a bad idea, but God instructed him to do it anyway, anointing a man named Saul from the tribe of Benjamin.

He started out well, acting in a very humble, unassuming manner, and actually seemed to accomplish some good things (a review of 1 Samuel 8:1–12:25). After a while, however, Saul got a "big head" and began ignoring the advice of wiser people (namely Samuel) and flatly disobeying the guidance of God.

At this point, God instructed Samuel to travel to Bethlehem to anoint David as king to eventually replace Saul. Samuel is likened to a modern day Billy Graham, and he was very well known throughout the country, which is amazing given the fact that there was no communication system like we enjoy today.

God didn't tell Samuel specifically who was designated as the next king, only that he was one of Jesse's sons, so upon arrival Jesse happily began parading his boys one by one before Samuel. Eliab, the eldest, was apparently rather tall, had a great physique ("do not consider his appearance or height") and must have *looked* kingly.

Samuel immediately liked what he saw and presumably opened his mouth to say something. God instantly stopped him. Something about the inner character of Eliab disqualified him for the job; although, nothing specific is given as to what that was.

JOSEPH RINEHART & BRENDA RINEHART

Interestingly enough, later in the story of David, Eliab scolds David for showing up as Goliath was challenging the Israelite army (1 Samuel 17:28), which may have indicated insecurity, jealousy, or other personal shortcomings.

David, as the youngest of eight brothers, was at the bottom of the proverbial food chain, to the point that it never even occurred to anyone even to invite him to meet Samuel. Ironically, at Samuel's insistence, David came and was clearly God's choice as the next ruler of the kingdom, though everything about the choice went against conventional wisdom.[2]

The critical truth in this passage is expressed as: "The LORD does not look at the things man looks at. Man looks at the outward appearance, but the LORD looks at the heart" (1 Samuel 17:13, NIV).

The Point:

In other words, as human beings, we have to rely primarily on the impressions that we get through our five senses: sight, smell, hearing, taste, and touch; while all five operate, sight and hearing are probably the primary means that most of us use. For example, first impressions usually shape our opinions of people we meet and interact with. Sometimes these can be faulty, but often they are hard to alter once fixed in our minds.

The problem is that what we can perceive can also be greatly flawed, and thus totally off base. In my comparatively brief life I have encountered many different individuals that I had drawn incorrect conclusions about. For those who read people well, your margin of error may be much lower than most, but we can all miss the mark and misread verbal cues, the actual meaning of words, and of course, intentions.

God sees everything—true intentions, motives, thoughts, fears, insecurities, perceptions, and every other unseen element of a human being. We, on the other hand, have to guess at these things based on what we perceive externally. Perception is an interesting thing because our perceptions are based on our own personal experiences—given the number of marital arguments, interpersonal conflicts, political infighting, and even wars, I would suggest that this process is limited at best and flawed at worst.

When you and I make a habit of interpreting the actions of others, we lack the necessary insight to truly understand them completely. If we start out with the assumption that we can easily misunderstand other people and equally misinterpret their actions, then it puts us in a better, more humble frame of mind.

> My brothers, as believers in our glorious LORD Jesus Christ, don't show favoritism. Suppose a man comes into your meeting wearing a gold ring and fine clothes, and a poor man in shabby clothes also comes in. If you show special attention to the man wearing fine clothes and say, "Here's a good seat for you," but say to the poor man, "You stand there" or "Sit on the floor by my feet," have you not discriminated among yourselves and become judges with evil thoughts?
>
> James 2:1–4 (NIV)

Background:

James was the half-brother of Jesus and one of the early leaders in the very first Christian church in Jerusalem and wrote one of the earliest books in the New Testament, the book that bears his name. Since Christianity began in Israel, naturally the first converts to the new movement were Jewish by birth and culture.

Things changed later during the first century when Paul, a later convert, traveled throughout the Roman Empire spreading the news about Christ, and to this very day the various flavors of Christianity are Gentile, which simply means non-Jew.

As with any group of imperfect human beings, the congregation in Jerusalem had certain issues they were dealing with, and this brief writing sought to address the major ones. From an economic standpoint, the church had members of varying backgrounds, some of whom possessed a substantial amount of material possessions and others who had very little. Acts 2:44 and 4:32 used the phrase "had all things common" to describe the practice of one family sharing with another within the congregation.

While this probably continued even into the period in which James wrote, he indicates that some of the members—and possibly even leaders—tended to treat some people differently. The well-dressed wealthy member of "First Jerusalem" apparently got the best seat in the house (perhaps like the box seats in modern sports stadiums). However, when someone showed up in jeans with holes in them and in beat-up shoes (so to speak), they were rudely told to stay out of the way and sit by the door. In other words, they ended up playing favorites and treating people differently.[3]

The Point:

Whether we want to admit it or not, we all have a tendency to treat people based on personal preferences; some are neutral, others are discriminatory and may reflect prejudice. Often we seek out other people with whom we share similar experiences, interests, viewpoints, opinions, and beliefs—sometimes called affinity groups because they center on similarities.

Preferences, opinions, and personal tastes have no true moral value, so they are neither right nor wrong, but sometimes we can end up excluding others simply because they do not belong to the "club." Segregation of races at one time played upon this whole concept and obviously demonstrated the extreme, but at times intelligent, modern, educated people can act in a very similar manner.

Treating someone from a similar background, race, or culture differently than someone from a less familiar one in essence "plays favorites." Looking down on those with illnesses, who may be homeless, or not well off also plays into the same mindset. Realizing that God created all human beings with equal value can help us act in a more even manner with other people.

> Do not judge, or you too will be judged. For in the same way you judge others, you will be judged, and with the measure you use, it will be measured to you. "Why do you look at the speck of sawdust in

your brother's eye and pay no attention to the plank in your own eye? How can you say to your brother, 'Let me take the speck out of your eye,' when all the time there is a plank in your own eye? You hypocrite, first take the plank out of your own eye, and then you will see clearly to remove the speck from your brother's eye.

Matthew 7:1–5 (NIV)

Background:

All four accounts of the life of Jesus (called the Gospels, gospel meaning "good news") were written around a certain theme and targeted to a specific readership. Matthew demonstrates the theme of Jesus as the promised Messiah and is targeted to the Jewish audience, as demonstrated by the many references to Old Testament prophecies and assumed understanding of religious and cultural traditions. Mark targeted to the Romans, as evidenced by its explanation of unfamiliar words and Jewish customs, its brief length, and its emphasis on action.

Luke targeted the Greeks, demonstrated by its thoroughness, citation of historical references, and many details, which would appeal to the intellectual mind. John targeted the believing Christian community of his day, and John sought in his writing to counter the false teachings that Jesus was either not fully human or not fully God. This specific account has a distinctly Jewish religious flavor, showing Jesus as a traveling teacher, in this case teaching near Jerusalem on the Mount of Olives.

Jesus instructed His followers not to make it their business to pass judgment on other people. The best way to understand this in its historical context is to look at the various religious groups operating in Israel during the time of Jesus.

The Sadducees represented the Jewish priesthood and had a great deal of political power; they would probably be described accurately as theologically more liberal in that they only accepted the books of Moses (Genesis, Exodus, Leviticus, Numbers, and Deuteronomy) and generally doubted the supernatural.

The Pharisees were the religiously conservative sect, very popular with the people, and rather zealous regarding the Old Testament. They were very quick to condemn "the unworthy" or "common sinners" because they did not follow the rather large number of made-up rules that they called doctrine.

Other groups existed and had encounters with Jesus, but these two were the most prominent; Jesus likely was referencing the judgmental and critical attitudes of these groups in this set of teachings. In later encounters, Jesus called the Pharisees out by name and attributed similar descriptions to them, which of course made them very angry.[4]

It is rather striking that Jesus spoke in gentle conciliatory terms with the spiritual outcasts of His own day but had scathing condemnation for the religious establishment! Specifically here, Jesus points out that those who point out small defects in others usually have managed to overlook the rather large shortcomings in their own lives.

The Point:

Taking on the practice of condemning others for their imperfections is self-defeating; first, because every human being on the planet makes mistakes, possesses character flaws, and does wrong, not just on occasion, but all the time. True, not everyone steals, acts in a disloyal manner, or murders others in cold blood, but chances are that they do, have done, or will do other things that wrong other people.

Individuals that feel they have the capacity, wisdom, and divine right to point out the faults of other people simply have their own hidden issues and problems. No one living escapes the simple fact that they make bad decisions. Jesus used the plain word *hypocrite* here—in ancient times, it referred to the performance of actors on the drama stage who held up masks to represent the character they were playing. In essence, when we presume to condemn, put down, or pass judgment on other people, we are hiding our *real* selves behind a mask and presenting ourselves as something we are not.

In the business world, I have seen this many times over the years and have affectionately termed this *B.S.*—not referring to farmland fertilizer directly, but rather calling it "business/bureaucratic storytelling." When we simply acknowledge the fact that we possess the same inherent weakness as every other person on the planet, this also serves to remind us that in this regard we are all "in the same boat," and no one is better than anyone else.

Questions

1. What are the biggest mistakes you have ever made in your life? If you have as many as I do, just pick the top three. Pick the top "mess up," and ask yourself the following questions about the experience:

   • How did that make me feel?

   • How did it make others involved feel?

   • Where did I really get off track with this?

   • What did I end up learning when all was said and done?

   • How did I use the experience to keep from making the same mistake again?

2. What "pet peeves" do you have that *really* tend to set you off? How do you typically respond to people that hit those triggers? Can you recall the last time that happened and how it turned out?

3. In what area(s) of your life do you feel weakest or least competent? When faced with that/those, how does that make you feel, and how do you react? Contrast that with area(s) in your life where you feel strongest/most capable. What potential dangers can/does that pose for you?

4. What is the difference between judgmental attitudes/actions and making valid evaluations? How would you explain that to your young child or a grown adult? Is there a difference?

5. Probably every one of us has dealt with overly critical people (those who pretend to know it all are very irritating to those of us who actually do!). Thinking of this specific person, think through the following:

    •   What makes them act this way? Why do they do this?

    •   How do I typically react when they do it?

    •   What price do they pay personally for acting this way?

    •   When have I acted in the same manner? How can I change that?

Prayer

LORD, please give me insight into my own faults, flaws, and issues when looking at the people I encounter in my life, whether friend or foe. Help me look at other people with the same love, compassion, and understanding that you did when you walked on the earth. Give me understanding when I observe the actions of others, and humility to understand the truth instead of assuming I am infallible. Let my actions reveal the truth of a loving, caring Father instead of a fierce judge. Help me make a positive difference where you have placed me in the world today and use my influence in ways that can make a difference. Most of all help me to see others through your eyes. In Jesus's name, Amen.

Hide and Seek: Personhood

A person is a person, no matter how small.

Horton the Elephant

Seeking is fun, but hiding is the point of the game, ultimately, who can outsmart whom. It was fun to play just about anywhere, but my most favorite time occurred when we moved into our newly constructed home a few days before Christmas.

The six-bedroom house was completely empty except for the only thing we had managed to unpack—a Christmas tree. The power was out in the entire region due to an ice storm, but the gas fireplace worked just fine to warm the place up. Our daughter gleefully proclaimed, "Wouldn't it be great to play hide and seek in here?" and without hesitation we all scampered away leaving her to be "it."

We all participated by climbing into window seats, closets, cupboards, and storage spaces until there were no more surprise hiding places left in the house, and we heard our last call of "All ye, all ye, in free!" yelled at a feverish pitch ...

— *Brenda*

A diagram: a pyramid divided into four horizontal levels. From top to bottom: **Acceptance**, **Cultural Values**, **Personal Values**, **Personhood**.

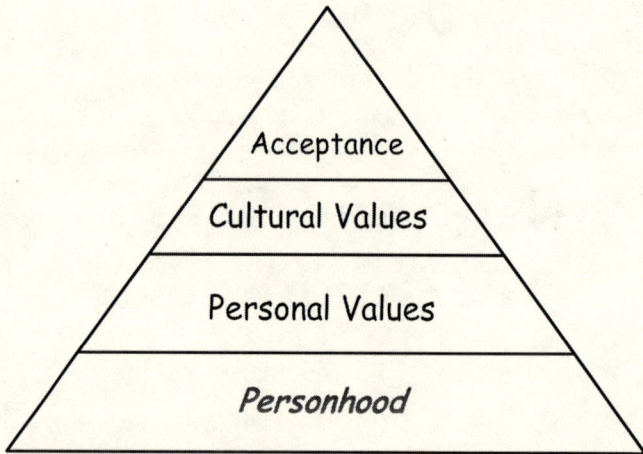

As a child in a single parent household, one of the tasks I loathed the most involved hanging framed portraits on the wall of our two-bedroom apartment. Sounds innocent enough, right? On the other hand, you might have to stand on a chair literally for hours hearing things like, "It's crooked; up more on the left," "No, it's too low," "Can't you get it centered?" "I don't like it there," and an entire plethora of other sound bites. Needless to say, rarely did I ever spend less than an hour pounding whatever nails I could find into the carpet we had hung on our living room wall—ah, suburban living!

One reason for despising that experience had to do with the tools at my disposal, or rather the lack of them. Seldom, if ever, did I find an actual hammer to drive the nails in; I had to settle for the handle of a screwdriver, a block of wood, a pair of vice grips, and my personal favorite—a pipe wrench!

Using the wrong tools for the right job may work in certain circumstances, but it goes against the fundamental design or "reason for being" of the implement in question. Understanding the intended purpose or design of something is key to achieving maximum efficiency in using it.

When in doubt, check with the manufacturer, or at least take the time to read the instructions, these days they come in at least four different languages!

Getting to the root of a judgmental attitude requires getting back to the foundational elements of why God, the Designer of man, created the human race to begin with. The best term to use in this context is *personhood*, namely "what it means to be a person or human being." The American Heritage Dictionary officially defines this as: "The state or condition of being a person, especially having those qualities that confer distinct individuality."[1]

Without this backdrop, understanding would prove difficult, if not impossible. The problem is that as humans, we frequently carry biases, preconceived notions, and assumptions that cloud our perception of issues and impair our ability to see things clearly. Grasping the objective truth regarding the intended design of humankind can provide a little perspective around the rest of the issues at hand. In essence, going back to the beginning sets the stage for correctly understanding everything else.

The opening chapter of the book of Genesis describes the beginning of human beings; God, the Creator, documents this momentous event with this simple statement: "So God created man in his own image, in the image of God he created him; male and female he created them" (Genesis 1:26, NIV).

The phrase that jumps off the page, so to speak, is "in the image of God." Scholars and theologians have debated the intended meaning of the wording literally for thousands of years with very little agreement between them. Some understand the "image" as pertaining to some physical resemblance to God, in much the same way that children typically carry resemblance to their parents.

Others view the concept as more relational, namely that only as humanity relates to the Creator does that image even exist. A more likely explanation identifies this "image of God" as certain inherent characteristics tied to the very essence and nature of human beings and marks them as unique in the entire created order.[2]

Taking that approach, then, it makes sense that these "fingerprints of God" exist naturally in every member of the human race and can be distinctly called out or identified. For the purpose of simplicity, we can call this "personhood" and answer the basic question of what constitutes a person or human being. In addition, it can help us gain a better grasp of how God designed humanity and what He actually had in mind in the first place.

While not exhaustive, these include self-awareness, self-determination or will, purpose, creativity, a spiritual nature, and intrinsic worth (Genesis 1:27–30, 2:7, 15–17). As amazing and wonderful as the universe and animals may be, the functional distance between them and humanity is substantial. For the purpose of this section, let's talk about self-determination and intrinsic worth specifically.

Self-determination, sometimes termed "free will" or independence, is one of the core concepts that nearly all members of the human race identify as essential to being a person. In modern times this was enshrined by movies like *The Matrix* (a personal favorite of mine) and in phrases like "the problem is choice." Historically, the Declaration of Independence identified this as the right to "life, liberty, and the pursuit of happiness" and formed the cornerstone of the fledgling government of the United States of America.

Going even further back, again looking at Genesis, God set this principle of choice in chapter 2, as follows: "And the Lord God commanded the man, 'You are free to eat from any tree in the garden; but you must not eat from the tree of the knowledge of good and evil, for when you eat of it you will surely die'" (Genesis 2:16–17, niv).

Once again, endless debate surrounds both this book and the verses contained in the earliest chapters. Usually this is surrounding the validity of the creation account, the actual existence of the garden of Eden, the historicity of Adam and Eve, and other aspects of the narrative. Focusing on those items exclusively ends up creating the situation of actually missing the whole point.

In reality, the central theme of this passage highlights the fact that choice was not only possible for human beings but an *essential design feature*. Without the capability to freely make decisions, humans would be little more than biological machines following instructions or animals guided by instinct. To understand how intrinsic self-determination is to personhood, one needs only to consult recorded history, and humanity's reaction to oppression, imprisonment, or enslavement.

The ability to make intelligent—or in some cases, not so intelligent—choices is central to personhood. As "persons" we make decisions every day, some fairly mundane, such as what route to take to work or whether to have a sandwich or a salad for lunch, and others which are life-changing and undeniably critical. As individuals, you and I choose a career, an educational institution, a spouse, whether to have children, ethical outcomes, and a myriad of other things.

This aspect of personhood highlights the vast gap between the human race and the rest of the beings that inhabit the planet. Animals, for example, act on instinct, and while some can make certain basic decisions, these pale in comparison to the complexity of human choices. A spider, for example, spins a web, a feat of engineering and a biological miracle that humans cannot equal. The ability and drive to make the web is hard-wired to the "programming" of the spider, not a carefully thought-out choice, which is often evidenced when my wife and I go hiking and have to clear them from the trail!

Humanity, on the other hand, sees a river, decides that for people to cross it a bridge has to be built, so they design it, procure the material, and build the structure. Rather than acting on pre-programmed responses, the builders demonstrated the ability to reason, analyze, and make decisions based on specific criteria.[3] Because of that ability, many people would say that this is the place where personal value is determined—our lives are the sum total of the choices we make.

While choice is paramount and the consequences of our choices may cause us great heartache, we indeed are not merely the sum total of our choices. According to our Creator we have an intrinsic worth because we are valuable to Him; if we were not, He certainly wouldn't have sacrificed His only Son for any of us. The mere fact that God took the time to create a being capable of independent thought and will, one that could choose to love Him back, and have a vital personal connection with Him, speaks volumes to the immense value endowed on humanity. This underscores the fact that human life possesses an innate value in and of itself, a point that very few of us actually grasp.

The concept of personhood places value on the individual human being apart from any real or potential achievements, economic value as a worker, personal value as a family member, or any act—good or bad—that they might do; this type of thinking runs contrary to the way most of us operate in life. We tend to look at other human beings in terms of what they can do for us or bring to our own experience.

In that respect humanity is also remarkably self-centered, namely, that we look at the universe and everything around us in terms of how it affects us personally. For example, can you recall a time when you were very young, when you may have missed a day of school, and in your own mind you thought none of your classmates went to school either simply because you were not there?

As we grow older, we get used to the idea that the world does not actually revolve around us, yet a part of us still maintains that how we see things is right, that our experiences are more valid, and that our beliefs are better than those belonging to someone else. When we truly grasp this core idea that every human being around us is unique, self-determining, and inherently valuable, only then can we can start to grasp that we can accept them as a person—validate their own personhood—regardless of their beliefs, viewpoints, and even behaviors. Only then do you and I function as the Designer made us, instead of turning into a clumsy tool that leaves scars and holes in the proverbial walls of other people's lives.

The second facet of the concept of personhood that we should consider is intrinsic worth, something that is vastly misunderstood and even more often misapplied. Since the dawn of time, we as human beings have tried to define our worth and value, and in collective societies we have promoted the value each person holds among one another. While not exhaustive by any means, the general categories are physical, positional, and productive.

Physical worth is surface-oriented in nature and probably one of the primary means by which a person is valued, both positively and negatively. Natural attractiveness and "sex appeal" play a major role in every society, as evidenced in the media: Actors, models, singers, and even political figures make use of good looks, and the companies promoting them often make a handsome profit doing it.

Bodily strength and agility are additional forms of physical worth and serve as the central point for professional athletes, gymnasts, dancers, and so on. Close on the heels of strength is personality, especially those that are at ease with people, confident, and easy to engage in conversation. Considering the addition of natural talents to this category almost sounds like the making of the prom king and queen of high school. Every social group has members within it that derive their worth and value from some form of innate physical capability.

Positional worth is not directly related to physical aspects of a person but can certainly follow it in some form. This group of values is derived from some type of relationship, position, or power. Using the example of high school again, those on sports teams or the cheerleading squad had social standing because of their affiliations. In the adult world it can manifest itself in membership of certain clubs, social groups, positions of influence, or power, that are often related to financial standing. The value attributed to these individuals is more external than innate.

Productive worth centers on an individual's ability to contribute to the society in which they live. In tribal cultures, the hunter has value to the clan because of the food he makes available to others, the farmer has value for similar reasons, and so forth. In modern times, those with strong work ethics have favor with their superiors and/or companies. Individuals with intelligence and the ability to apply that intelligence and those with creative gifts also have value because of what they can produce, create, or bring to a group.

All of the systems of value described above, while true to life, have immense pitfalls that life has a way of bringing up. The "beautiful people" age and lose their glamour, or they may suffer an accident or illness that nullifies that advantage entirely. Power and popularity can vanish in an instant, and even a job or career can end in seconds.

Keep in mind while these valuations may be reflected in the opinions of society that society is composed of people who choose to buy into that thought process, and as individuals we tend to buy into it ourselves. The heart of the issue lies in the fact that every one of those systems of value rely on what a person *has* or *can do* not on who they *are*, or more specifically, *Whose* they are!

By virtue of creation, human beings carry the very imprint of God within them, separating them from and exalting them above the rest of the created order. This very fact alone, along with other indications in the biblical record, ascribes great worth and value apart from any actions, possessions, natural talents, or position an individual may have.[2]

This sentiment is echoed throughout documents such as the Declaration of Independence, with words such as "that all men are created equal" and invoked in modern times through visionary leaders like Dr. Martin Luther King, Jr. Even the most casual reading of the Genesis narrative shouts out the significance of the inauguration of human life in the most majestic of terms. However, history and experience paint a portrait of mankind that is anything but kind.

In many instances, the created order of the human race is a profound study in contrasts. Artists, sculptors, musicians, and builders over the eons of time have created breathtaking art, music, and physical structures that can awe and inspire. In contrast, one group has attempted genocide against others; the powerful have oppressed the weak, and the greatest atrocities imaginable have been committed daily by one human being against another.

How can the truth communicated by the concept of intrinsic value be squared up against the plain truth of historical experience? The answer lies in the finite and imperfect nature of humanity.

At first glance that sounds like it starkly contradicts the entire argument of the previous section, although in reality it affirms it. Like everything else, the truths have to be considered in the right context. Early Greek mythology attempted to explain the obvious reality of an imperfect world as the direct fault of the curious Pandora, who opened the forbidden box and introduced evil into the world.

Regardless of the actual source, stories like these point to the fact that no one experiences life free of imperfection. In the context of Genesis, God gave a pretty specific prohibition to the newly created man and woman: "But you must not eat from the tree of the knowledge of good and evil, for when you eat of it you will surely die" (Genesis 2:17, NIV).

Nothing in this passage indicates how much time passed between the initial warning and the eventual violation, but the effects of that decision were immediate—alienation from one another as well as God, disruption in the entire created order, and the eventual end of physical life.

Aside from the imperfect nature of people, another important fact to understand is the finite nature of humanity as well. The Merriam-Webster dictionary defines finite as "having definite or definable limits; having a limited nature or existence." Today, the lifespan of a human being is sixty to eighty years, with the undisputed record being 122, a French woman named Jeanne Calment (who died in 1997).[3]

Regardless of the range, the fact is that our lifespan is certainly limited; we are born unable to fend for ourselves, we learn and grow, age, and eventually expire. If we do not accomplish everything within our lifetime, it simply does not happen—unlike tax returns, there is no ability to appeal or apply for an extension. As mentioned previously, human ingenuity and creativity is amazing—another aspect of the image of God—but it still bears the marks of limitations.

Technology solves many problems but then creates others. Wonder drugs and medications treat many diseases and yet cause side effects (I am continually amazed at the thirty-second legal disclaimers in most drug commercials). Systems of government, economics, labor, education, business, travel, and such are all plainly limited and imperfect at best; failing to acknowledge that fact is ridiculous and self-defeating.

Additionally, human intellect demonstrates limits, regardless of how bright a particular mind may be. Using the analogy of a container, the mind can only hold so much before reaching its capacity. Some containers may be larger than others, but they still have limits.[6]

What is the ultimate point of the concept of personhood? First, humanity stands apart from the rest of the creatures on the planet as majestic—endowed by the Creator with the power of free choice, possessing intrinsic personal worth and potential, but still limited and capable of very destructive, self-centered, and shortsighted actions. Think of this entire concept as the first link in the chain of understanding where judgmental attitudes come from. Seeing human beings from this perspective is the first step in being able to better relate to others, even when they may come across as less than ideal.

Going Deeper

Then God said, "Let us make mankind in our image, in our likeness, so that they may rule over the fish in the sea and the birds in the sky, over the livestock and all the wild animals,[a] and over all the creatures that move along the ground." So God created mankind in his own image, in the image of God he created them; male and female he created them.

Genesis 1:26–27 (NIV)

Background:

As discussed previously, God created human beings very differently than the rest of creation, including angels. According to Psalm 148:1–5, God created angels presumably before the events recounted in the early chapters of Genesis, though not many details are supplied.

In Genesis 2:7, the Bible speaks of God *breathing* life into the human form, which is in stark contrast to the language of "let there be…" used prior to that, with regard to the world itself, and in relation to other creatures. The "image of God," which man possesses, as previously discussed, had several characteristics (not exhaustive), such as:

1.   Self-Awareness

   •   One of the obvious features presented in the Genesis account, as well as the general human experience, is the concept of self-awareness. Human beings have the ability to see themselves as individual beings apart from everything around them, including social units (families, tribes, clans, etc.), other creatures (animals, birds, fish, etc.), and the physical environment (the ground, the sky, vegetation, etc.).

   •   While a person may not always fully grasp *who* they are (individual gifts, traits, and capacities), they do know *what* they are. This can be reinforced by the idea that when a human being fails to be self-aware it is usually attributed to a brain-related issue such as an injury, mental illness, or other condition).

2. Self-Determination or Will (previously considered)

- Another prominent feature of the opening chapters of Genesis is the enablement of self-will or the ability to make personal choices. God's prohibition regarding the "forbidden fruit" actually highlights the fact that choice was, not only possible for human beings, but an essential design feature.

- Without the capability to freely make decisions, humans would be little more than biological machines following instructions or animals guided by instinct. To understand how intrinsic self-determination is to personhood one needs only to consult recorded history and humanity's reaction to oppression, imprisonment, or enslavement.

3. Purpose

- God clearly created the human race with multifaceted purposes in mind, including the intention to work, procreate, build, create, and enjoy relationships, most importantly with God Himself. One of the universal truths echoed in just about every religion throughout the world is the concept that man was created on purpose, for a purpose.

- General principles can certainly apply to the entire species, as previously mentioned, but the unique individual abilities, personalities, and inclinations also dictate a much more personal and individual sense of purpose as well. Again, history, particularly in the United States, can easily verify this "hard wired" characteristic as part of what it means to be a person.

4. Creativity

- Within the various individual members of the human race lies an amazing range of personal abilities, talents, and resources. Humans are the only species of being on the planet that engage in creative work such as art, music, architecture, philosophy, and other such outlets.

- Even the more "mundane" tasks such as construction of roads and bridges reflect a totally unique ability to make things. The animal kingdom shows no shortage of creatures that build, march, fight, and such, but none show the creative aspect that human beings innately possess.

5. Spiritual Nature

- God clearly intended humans to actively and willingly participate in an intimate relationship with Him. The almost universal existence of belief in God among the species and the vast proliferation of religions of all types throughout all of recorded history certainly attest to that. Ironically, in an age where so much rational thought challenges any idea of faith, religion still exists and even thrives.

- While debate may exist as to the validity of one belief system over another, the pervasiveness of the belief itself points to the fact that it is yet another essential element of personhood.

6. Intrinsic Worth (previously considered)

- God took the time to desire, design, create, and empower humanity as the only being on the planet capable of self-awareness, choice, purpose, creativity, and spiritual awareness. The mere fact that God created humanity instills the race, with all its faults and shortcomings, with tremendous personal and individual worth.

- In addition, the elements of personhood described above also in and of them have value. Understanding that this is intrinsic to personhood and not tied to what that person has/has not done is a very powerful concept that should empower anyone to know that human life by its very nature has immeasurable value.

The Point:

Human beings, as previously discussed, carry immense personal value based on the fact that they are a special creation by God Himself; man was not an afterthought or byproduct but the goal of the created order. In relationship to the specific topic in this chapter, as previously mentioned, the value of any individual human being is entirely separate from their actions and/or behaviors.

One of the many clichés repeated in many Christian churches is, "Love the sinner, hate the sin," and the intention is to communicate the concept that a *person* should always be shown consideration and respect, even if their *actions* fall short of God's standards. In reality, a lot of "religious folk" of all walks of life have a hard time distinguishing between the two, and the impression that people get is that they look down on them.

In literally every encounter between Jesus and everyday people, He looked past whatever their immediate situation was right to their actual need. He consistently treated them with affirmation, respect, and acceptance without once condoning behaviors or lifestyles that He did not agree with. Christ's gentle words, "Go and sin no more," never carried the harsh tone of condemnation, though it did urge living a new life altogether.

> So then, about eating food sacrificed to idols: We know that an idol is nothing at all in the world and that there is no God but one. For even if there are so-called gods, whether in heaven or on earth (as indeed there are many "gods" and many "lords"), yet for us there is but one God, the Father, from whom all things came and for whom we live; and there is but one LORD, Jesus Christ, through whom all things came and through whom we live. But not everyone knows this. Some people are still so accustomed to idols that when they eat such food they think of it as having been sacrificed to an idol, and since their conscience is weak, it is defiled … For if anyone with a weak conscience sees you who have this knowledge eating in an idol's temple, won't he be emboldened to eat what has been sacrificed to idols? So this weak brother, for whom Christ died, is destroyed by your knowledge. When you sin against your brothers in this way and wound their weak conscience, you sin against Christ …
>
> 1 Corinthians 8:4–13 (NIV)

Background:

Paul, one of the most prominent leaders of the early Christian church, started out actually hunting down the followers of Jesus, imprisoning and, in some cases, arranging their execution. While traveling to the city of Damascus in Syria, Paul had an encounter with the risen Christ, resulting in his conversion to the new movement.

During his travels throughout the Roman Empire, Paul started churches in various cities, including the city of Corinth in Greece. Corinth had a rather negative reputation since it possessed a culture that indulged rather thoroughly in lifestyles that would have made the sixties look tame by comparison.

A case in point was the temple to the goddess Aphrodite where a thousand ritual prostitutes regularly made themselves available to worshipers. The church in Corinth was in fact founded by Paul himself (Acts 18:1–18), composed of both Jewish and Gentile membership, and suffered some of the same moral issues that the city itself was famous for.

This mixed background of the church in Corinth sets the stage for the problem raised by Paul in the passage above. Several of the local pagan temples would sacrifice animals to their particular deity and rather than waste the meat, would essentially sell it at a discount. Certain members of the church didn't care about where the meat came from, and would buy it and eat it without as much as a second thought.

Keep in mind that further back in their history, the Jews had indulged rather deeply in idol worship, to the point that it corrupted their religious practices, and God allowed them to be exiled as a result; needless to say, they maintained a certain sensitivity to idol worship from that point on. In this example, upon hearing about some members of the church getting their steaks and hamburgers from the temple of Aphrodite they were rather upset, and it caused quite a stir.

Paul makes the point that idols actually are just dead religious furniture and that as such the meat was not in and of itself somehow spiritually suspect, while at the same time he points out that the Corinthian believers needed to put the feelings and needs of others ahead of their own.[7]

The Point:

To my knowledge, this specific issue of eating meat from "Aphrodite's Deli" is not one facing members of modern Christian denominations. More likely, the topics of concern would center on the use of alcohol, styles of worship, involvement in politics, music, and similar issues. If you look at the history of religion, the most acrid splits have seldom been over substantial issues but more often over non-essential items.

Entire congregations have scattered over the color of carpet, whether or not to have stained glass windows, how the furniture is arranged, and other utterly silly reasons. Truth be told, there are many legitimate areas of disagreement that can happen on numerous issues, but the problem is that when a person feels strongly about one, it becomes far too easy to personalize it. Instead, Christ wants us to put the needs, feelings, and others ahead of our own and treat them in a loving manner regardless of our differences.

So all the elders of Israel gathered together and
came to Samuel at Ramah. They said to him, "You
are old, and your sons do not walk in your ways;
now appoint a king to lead us, such as all the other
nations have." But when they said, "Give us a king
to lead us," this displeased Samuel; so he prayed
to the LORD. And the LORD told him: "Listen to
all that the people are saying to you; it is not you
they have rejected, but they have rejected me as
their king."

1 Samuel 8:4–7 (NIV)

Background:

Prior to the inauguration of the monarchy under Saul, and,
later, David, the nation of Israel was governed by rulers
called the judges (for a period lasting around 300 years
roughly). These leaders typically came on the stage during
some period when an enemy nation was oppressing Israel,
remained in power for a time, and passed off the scene.

Government during this time did not have a highly
formal system of any kind, fragmenting the ability of
Israel to respond to outside threats as well as internal strife
within its own borders. As a result, political and cultural
chaos existed throughout the nation, and society as a whole
degenerated into corruption and, as a result, nearly wiped
out an entire segment of the country.

Samuel, the final judge/ruler of this period, served a
rather long time and had considerable political, spiritual,
and military influence that brought significant stability.
Even so, representatives of the various tribes and clans of

Israel clamored for him to set up a monarchy, insisting that this alone would ensure long-term stability, prosperity, and protection from neighboring enemy nations.

At first Samuel was indignant and, probably being an outspoken individual, very likely gave a stern response to the request. Oddly enough, God spoke to Samuel, indicating that he should heed their request and the decision they had made collectively. Included in the instructions to establish the Israelite monarchy, however, God told the prophet to issue a warning about the drawbacks that would come with the kingship. In the final analysis, the people of Israel flatly ignored the warning and stood firm on their request for a king.[8]

The Point:

Biblical history records numerous examples of individuals, nations, and groups of people making ill-advised decisions that led to unpleasant consequences—Abraham "helped" God to give him a son and heir (Ishmael) that grew into an adversary for Isaac, who was born later. Isaac played favorites with his sons, which ended up not only causing conflict between the brothers, but conflict between the nations that both men fathered.

The nation of Israel later stood ready to enter the Promised Land less than four years after leaving Egypt as slaves and then chose to turn back. Humanity's ability to choose carries with it both positive, as well as negative possibilities, as both biblical and secular history have amply recorded.

Another striking feature of the ability to choose, however, is God's acceptance of the choices of the beings He created. While God certainly knows the best use of the life He designed for every one of us, and compassionately tries to guide as best as possible, He also still honors our will and our choices. As mentioned previously, the ability to freely choose is one of the great hallmarks of personhood, what it means to be human, made in the image of God.

Questions

1. Think of people in your life that you admire. What specifically do you admire about them and why? What personal characteristics or elements from their lives have you tried to emulate and why?

2. Think of people in your life that you deeply dislike. What specifically do you not like about them and why? What personal characteristics or elements from their lives have you tried to emulate the opposite of and why? Examine what you admire and dislike; how much of that is tied to things people do rather than who they are personally?

3. List out the five top achievements in your life that you are proudest of or feel the best about. How many of those can be affected by external circumstances or situations beyond your control?

4. How much of your self-esteem ends up wrapped up in these types of external factors? How can the essential elements of the concept of personhood create personal value beyond these tentative aspects of your life?

5. How can you look differently at the people you listed in response to question two with reference to their intrinsic value to God? Does that change anything about their choices and behaviors? Why or why not?

Prayer

LORD, give me new eyes to see other people as your unique creations—created and loved deeply by you. Give me the strength to look past the surface to the heart of the people I come across on the street, at work, or in unexpected encounters. Help me to look at myself as your creation, and please guide my choices. Please help me to actually listen when you try to guide me. Give me patience and understanding when I see the flaws in others and help me realize and forgive my own shortcomings. Help me to feel humility rather than arrogance. Grant me the courage to accept the things—and people—that I cannot change, the courage to change the things I can—in myself, through your power—and the wisdom to know the difference. In Jesus's name, Amen.

Duck, Duck, Goose: Personal Values

If you don't know where you are going, any road will get you there.

Lewis Carroll, Author of *Alice in Wonderland*

Can you remember kindergarten—the land of edible paste, Play-Doh, stories read out loud, and fun little games that were inspired by the "lesson" attached to them? In my kindergarten class we played an inside game right before naptime. Duck, Duck, Goose and musical chairs were two of my favorites.

The difference between the two was that in musical chairs the music was in control of how the game went; in Duck, Duck, Goose, I was in charge of my own choices. To win at Duck, Duck, Goose I had to be strategic in my choices. I couldn't just pick my favorite person; in fact, the goal was to be strategic enough to outrun your choice of "goose" entirely...

— *Brenda*

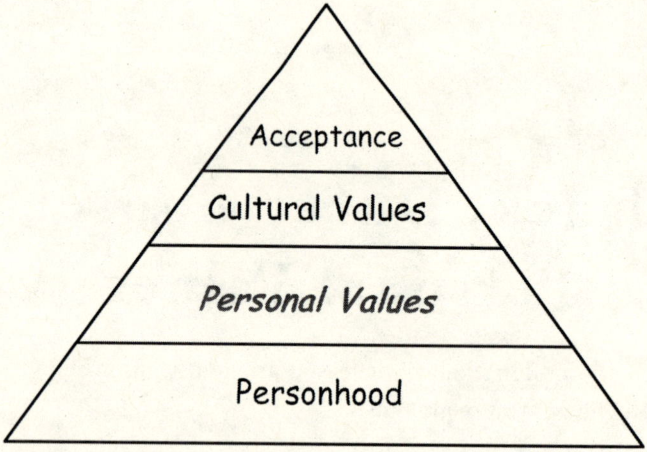
Acceptance
Cultural Values
Personal Values
Personhood

I *hate* raisins. I hate everything about them—the taste, the color, the texture, and every other aspect of their miserable existence. Soggy bread may come in as a close second, but there are fewer things that I despise more than raisins. I will be the first to admit that this intense dislike isn't rational. I didn't choke on them as a child, they were not forced on me at school, nor was I somehow tortured with them; it's simply a matter of personal preference.

Having said that, I feel obligated to share the fact that I distinctly recall one summer actually consuming them. My cousin Erik had invited me to serve as part of his wedding party as a groomsman, and I had hitched a ride with his best man, who happened to be in Florida at the time. During the course of our travels to Cincinnati, we had dinner with the best man's sister, all of which was perfectly acceptable until she sat some sort of spice cake on the table. I remember praying that it had no raisins in it, and I was instantly horrified to discover that in fact the dessert was *infested* with the nasty little buggers!

Not wanting to be rude, I tried discreetly eating around them, and when that didn't work, I swallowed them whole to avoid tasting them. Apparently they discovered my plan and showed up in force—large clumps of them—that I simply couldn't get past. Fortunately, at that point I could truthfully say that I was full, so I was able to deliver myself from almost certain death!

So what made me subjugate my fear and loathing of dried grapes? Simply put, I happen to hold politeness and consideration in high regard, as well as simple appreciation of a person's hospitality, and I chose that over my revulsion of dried fruit. I made a personal choice in that matter, exactly the way all of us do with various situations every day.

In the previous chapter we looked at the whole idea of personhood, namely, the idea of what God intended when He created the human race, and the fact that by design we have infinite individual worth and the capacity of self-determination. One of my favorite movies of all time, *The Matrix*, echoes the theme of choice as one of the cornerstones of the human experience.

Stopping at that point leaves an incomplete picture of truly understanding how so many people form such strong opinions that manifest themselves as judgmental attitudes. The larger panoramic view of the human experience requires taking the next logical step in the process, understanding the dynamics of personal values.

In the current state of the economy most of us have gained an entirely new appreciation of the concept of value; homes have lost value relative to the market, but still having a job in these tough times has value. For some, making the most money possible has value, for others it may be a flexible schedule that allows them to spend time with their family.

The entire free market economy spends literally billions of dollars yearly convincing consumers that their products and/or services bring some tangible value that merits surrendering money to obtain. In fact, we all make numerous decisions daily based on some perception of value, some that could be as explicit as right and wrong, and others that are between what is good and better.

In essence, whether we openly admit it or not, we live our individual lives on the basis of a system of values that we have chosen. In fact, this serves as a logical extension of the concept of self-determination that is an essential part of what it means to be a human being.

Immediately after creating humanity with the ability to freely choose, God tested that ability with a simple test, reflected in Genesis 2:16–17:

> And the LORD God commanded the man, "You are free to eat from any tree in the garden; but you must not eat from the tree of the knowledge of good and evil, for when you eat of it you will surely die."

In chapter three, Eve listened to the words of the serpent and ate the fruit, and ultimately humanity chose to go their own way rather than God's. Ever since that time, the human race has "tried on" numerous value systems, philosophies, and schools of thought upon which to base better decision-making, and that has trickled down into our own individual lives as well.

You and I choose values on a variety of factors, typically influenced by family, personal experience, popular culture, preferences, and nature, each of which is worthy of further consideration.

Family

The first classroom of learning for any human being is that of their family of origin, both in what is explicitly taught as well as what is implicitly modeled. The well-known passage, "Children Learn What They Live," by Dorothy Nolte, illustrates this rather vividly with the words, "If children live with criticism, they learn to condemn."

Values learned from family often fall into several categories—those we consciously embrace and choose to emulate, those we oppose and strive to live the opposite of, and those we unconsciously adopt because of familiarity. I will never forget the day that I discovered just how true these were.

I remember as a young child detesting when my mother would ask me to come here, and when I failed to do so, she would begin counting from one to three, in the stern "mommy voice" that could level city blocks or freeze fire (every living being, particularly males, know both "the look" and "the voice"). In the full hearing of my mom I declared unwaveringly that no child of mine would ever have to endure such "drama." That is, until some twenty or so years later when I ran out of patience with my oldest daughter, Naomi, who was a toddler and would not come when called. I found my lips forming the words, "One ... two ..." and before getting to three, an unhappy child came my way with a surly frown pasted on her face. On the one hand I was aghast that I did indeed what I had vowed never to do, but on the other hand, I was thinking, *Oh my goodness, it actually does work!*

The simple fact of the matter is that life within a family profoundly shapes our behaviors, personalities, and, yes, our values. Rituals, traditions, attitudes, values, practices, and other influences, while not innately burned into our DNA, nonetheless do end up ingrained into the adults we end up becoming. Understanding that fact, whether positive or negative, can help us better refine our value system.

Personal Experience

The second greatest set of influences that shape our personal values come from the real-time experiences in our lives, typically significant occurrences. Some of these could conceivably include life-changing events such as a childhood divorce, loss of a sibling or close relative, a near-death experience (such as almost drowning), popularity (or the lack of it) at school or work, and so on.

For example, Brenda, my wife, had a brother Danny to whom she was very close; their early childhood years were filled with chaos and instability, and they learned to rely on one another. At nine years old, Danny was diagnosed with leukemia, which grew progressively worse, and a short two years later he passed away.

As a result of experiencing that loss as a child, Brenda felt compelled to choose a career in the health-care profession, in order to make a difference in the lives of people; that specific personal experience led her to make choices that affected the path of her life later on.

Popular Culture

A third significant source of influence regarding personal values comes from the ever-present and always-changing world of popular culture; while in the United States we often appear to be the primary society that sways to the siren song of this influence, the rest of the world just has a different tune, so to speak.

I recall in the 1970s when *Saturday Night Fever* came out starring John Travolta, that disco music (courtesy of the Bee Gees), dancing, and dress all took off like wildfire! As with many trends, disco eventually ran its course and died out, giving way to other stars, movies, and ideas of what was "cool." Values based on pop culture constantly change and shift, making for an unstable foundation for living.

Preferences

The fourth general set of influences that lead us to choose our personal values have to do with personal tastes and preferences. Ironically, these are probably the least rational and have more to do with what we like than anything else. Music is a great example of this.

As a former pastor, I have been "entertained" by the strong assertion of other church leaders about the acceptable form of music that God has sanctioned; of course the acceptable form of music usually corresponded to that particular person's preference rather than on some biblical revelation on the subject.

In all honesty, I have heard some rather interesting arguments regarding the "right" style of music, some centering on the specific type of downbeat (which mainly ruled out rock music), others sternly maintaining that so-called secular music was not fit for church (in which case a lot of hymns would technically have to be banned).

Nature

The fifth and final source of potential values comes from human nature—a potentially controversial notion, which is why we consider it last in the list. Nearly every culture throughout the world and spanning history has a consistent core set of values in common; some writers refer to them as transcendent values because they exist outside the boundaries of any one group of human relationships.

While not totally precise, these values are found in most major religions (the Ten Commandments in Judaism have similarities in both the Christian Bible and Muslim Qur'an, for example) and focus on such things as marital fidelity, respect for property, and acknowl-edgement of deity. An example would be the parallels between the Ten Commandments in Judaism and moral teachings in the Christian Bible and Muslim Qur'an. Furthermore, even the examination of fairly primitive cultures, such as the Wayana Indians of South America, yield similar results; Dr. Ivan Schoen, longtime mis-sionary to this group, discovered this during his time among them.

Although the concept of transcendent or innate val-ues may not have universal acceptance, their existence indicates what Paul wrote in Romans 2 when he com-mented that the non-Jewish world showed "the law of God written in their hearts."

Each of us, based on any combination of these influ-ences, consciously chooses the system of values, which drives our decision-making processes, and ultimately, our lives. Some of them may be simply verbalized, others may be subtler, but ultimately the best judge of true values lies in demonstrated behavior—what we *do*, more than simply what we *say*.

For example, many individuals make strong state-ments about the importance of commitment to family but fail to demonstrate it in everyday interactions. The Arnold Schwarzenegger Christmas movie *Jingle All the Way* portrayed a father with the best of intentions, who had to face the fact that his values were quite misaligned.

A close examination of where a person invests their resources (usually money and time) yields another clue to what their values truly are. Jesus said, "Where your treasure is, your heart is also."

Not only do we choose the values we live by, but we also choose the order of their priority; *personal values have a distinct hierarchy*. In all likelihood, the list of values would rank the most critical at the top, with every value beneath not only dependent on that original value, but somehow less significant. At the bottom of the "list of what's important" the relative importance of the values can be remarkably casual. When values conflict, the ones higher on the list take precedence and overrule one or more of the lower ones.

Think of it like the court system of the United States—not perfect, but certainly practical and functional. Some cases are settled at the city or county level without much fuss; more important ones are appealed to a higher level for arbitration or decision. When the issue is significant enough, the Supreme Court gets involved, which may rescind the decisions already made and mandate a completely different direction.

The core principles of an individual's value system represent the highest decision-making criteria and, like the Supreme Court, usually serve throughout life. Values at the "lower court" level, by contrast, evolve and change over time, sometimes significantly. A well-known example of this principle is Abraham Maslow's "Hierarchy of Needs"—in that paradigm, specific basic human needs for self-preservation trump other needs in the hierarchy.

So why on earth talk about values when discussing judgmental attitudes? Simply put, *values feed attitudes and motivate actions*, all of which affect the interactions between one human being and another. For example, I spent the better part of ten years as a vocational pastor, from very rural settings to metropolitan communities, and interacted with numerous people from all backgrounds and walks of life.

Invariably I encountered individuals who had either had a negative church experience or a remarkably sour encounter with someone who regularly attended some religious group. When I was a young pastor in western Tennessee, a young couple that I visited with told me a story about a local pastor that had come to their home along with another member of the church.

This young couple had been divorced and remarried. Because of their personal history, the pastor felt compelled to warn them of swift and stern judgment by God, insisting that it could affect the lives and well-being of their family. To make his point, the man who had come with the pastor, told a story about how his infant child had died at birth, as punishment from God for his misdeeds.

No matter how well intentioned, the interaction indisputably offended the young couple and gave them a dark view not only of that church, but all churches.

Unfortunately, stories just like that are recounted in staggering numbers. Jesus, undeniably the founder and inspiration for Christian faith, operated in an entirely different manner than the tone depicted in stories like this one. Jesus didn't repel people; people were drawn to Him.

In biblical times, people flocked to Jesus. When He spoke to the woman at the well in John 13, He spoke to her without any condemnation of her lifestyle, worship of God, or anything else, but instead spoke to her with courtesy and respect. Clearly He did not condone or agree with many of the things she believed, but He still interacted with her willingly.

In stark contrast, He clashed with the Jewish religious leaders and had a great deal to say about their version of spiritual values. Jesus made it clear that enduring and stable personal values came *first* from loving God (Matthew 22:37) and then loving *people* (Matthew 22:38).

The whole discussion of values indicates that part of the issue is basic arithmetic; by virtue of having the ability to choose, we select our own individual values, which seldom, if ever, equate to the value system that another person holds. To express this quandary, the mathematical equation would look something like:

$$V = V_p + V_c$$

Values	Personal Values	Cultural Values

V stands for *values*, the collection of both *personal values* (as discussed here), and *cultural values*, the topic of the next chapter. These two sets of standards form the way that one looks at the world, themselves, and other people. In addition, value systems between human beings are often vastly dissimilar, mathematically expressed as:

$$V_{(1)} \neq V_{(2)}$$

My   Your

Values   Values

Ultimately, being created in God's image and having the ability to choose our own value system is both a blessing and a curse; choice is powerful, but when left to its own devices creates questionable value systems. This is the point at which judgmental attitudes can start.

Going Deeper

Hearing that Jesus had silenced the Sadducees, the Pharisees got together. One of them, an expert in the law, tested him with this question: "Teacher, which is the greatest commandment in the Law?" Jesus replied: " 'Love the LORD your God with all your heart and with all your soul and with all your mind.' This is the first and greatest commandment. And the second is like it: 'Love your neighbor as yourself.' All the Law and the Prophets hang on these two commandments."

Matthew 22:34–40 (NIV)

Background:

The Jewish religious establishment, particularly in Jerusalem, had identified Jesus as a threat almost from the beginning of His public teaching ministry. Aside from the simple fact that He was controversial, their viewpoint was that His teachings were contrary to their particular stances on just about everything.

Interestingly enough, these groups had clashes with John the Baptist previously, and the most strident exchanges between Christ and anyone else happened with them as well. The members of these religious sects were highly educated, well versed in the Old Testament writings, and steeped in commentaries interpreting these same writings.

In their eyes, they had the backing of long-established academic scholarship, the religious history spanning substantial amounts of time, and the blessing of the local people that revered their standing in the community.

Jesus, by contrast, had never attended rabbinical schools of any kind, was virtually unknown, and frankly paid no attention to the accepted traditions that they held dear. More than once, the Pharisees (one of the sects of the time) had approached Jesus publicly with well-crafted questions that represented no-win scenarios in an attempt to trap Him in some kind of dilemma.

Comically, Jesus always had a quick response that steered clear of any and every theological land mine they came up with. In this particular account, they wanted Jesus to prioritize the commandments and pick the most important one—keep in mind that the writings of that time had gone beyond the obvious Ten Commandments and had interpreted about 613 additional rules (according to the Talmud).

Obviously it would be difficult for any man to pick out the most important just based on the sheer number, especially while under pressure and in public no less, especially since it was an obvious trap—the one asking the question had advanced degrees in the subject! But they were dealing with Jesus!

Jesus, in His classic style, bypassed the spiritual and political implication of the questions and turned the entire thought process upside down, and He did so by making a reference to the most important principle of Judaism, called the Shema, declaring: "Hear, O Israel: The LORD our God, the LORD is One" (Deuteronomy 6:4). The very next phrase in the Old Testament is the one quoted by Christ—"love your neighbor as yourself"—indicating that above all else, God must be the first and foremost priority in a person's relationships.

At that point the Pharisee challenging Him may have been surprised but would have agreed with the statement (Luke's account records this in fact), but the second statement regarding loving one's neighbor would have thrown him a curve—these individuals were not known for their compassion.[1]

The Point:

As mentioned previously, the content of our value system does not exist in a vacuum, but has to come from *somewhere*. Without some sort of solid foundation or anchor, an individual can find themselves thrown about much like a ship in a fierce storm. Catch phrases such as "scientifically proven," "the latest survey," "top-rated studies," and so forth present frequently contradictory information, as well as trends in culture, education, and work environments.

In business, for example, companies that change their strategy frequently often find themselves in bankruptcy, taken over by a competitor, or marginalized in their sphere of influence. In the same way, you and I as human beings were designed to make choices, and those choices always depend on some system of personal values.

Since the world around us changes daily, if not hourly, we have a deep-seated need to build our priorities on something solid that does not change—the reason that Jesus emphasized the need to "love God with all your heart, mind, soul and strength."

In numerous other places through the Bible, God is described as truthful, steady, unchanging, dependable, constant, and eternally certain. In contrast to human beings, circumstances, and the world around us, God never changes! Tying our values, priorities, and decision-making processes to our "Manufacturer's Best Practice Recommendations" enables us to experience the very best in an imperfect world. The validity and strength of that relationship vertically (toward God) also must inevitably be demonstrated horizontally, namely toward other human beings also made in His image.

Following with what Jesus Himself taught, a faith that fails to demonstrate and practice a loving regard for others is inherently defective or incomplete. This can require us to examine what we have chosen to value and may be painful at times but represents the best possible way to truly live out the life that Jesus intended for us, and to live that out toward others in our lives as well.

Now Laban had two daughters; the name of the older was Leah, and the name of the younger was Rachel. Leah had weak eyes, but Rachel was lovely in form, and beautiful. Jacob was in love with Rachel and said, "I'll work for you seven years in return for your younger daughter Rachel." Laban said, "It's better that I give her to you than to some other man. Stay here with me." So Jacob served seven years to get Rachel, but they seemed like only a few days to him because of his love for her. Then Jacob said to Laban, "Give me my wife. My time is completed, and I want to lie with her." So Laban brought together all the people of the place and gave a feast. But when evening came, he took his daughter Leah and gave her to Jacob, and Jacob lay with her. And Laban gave his servant girl Zilpah to his daughter as her maidservant. When morning came, there was Leah! So Jacob said to Laban, "What is this you have done to me? I served you for Rachel, didn't I? Why have you deceived me?" Laban replied, "It is not our custom here to give the younger daughter in marriage before the older one. Finish this daughter's bridal week; then we will give you the younger one also, in return for another seven years of work." And Jacob did so. He finished the week with Leah, and then Laban gave him his daughter Rachel to be his wife.

Genesis 29:16–28 (NIV)

Background:

Jacob became a fugitive from his own home because his brother, Esau, had taken out a contract on his life. At that point Jacob fled the country and ended up taking refuge back in the "old country" (modern-day Iraq) with his relatives who still lived there. Laban was his uncle, more specifically, Rebekah's brother, and gladly took Jacob in and set him up with a decent job. Jacob was very attracted to Rachel, Laban's younger daughter, and agreed to work for him for seven years in exchange for her hand in marriage, to which Laban agreed.

Keep in mind that just like credit card purchases, the "transaction" (marriage) happened first, and the payment came later (the seven years of work). Just like a hotshot pool room hustler, Jacob found himself "out-hustled" by Laban when he woke up the morning after the wedding to see Leah, the older sister, rather than Rachel. At first thought, you might wonder how Jacob managed to miss something so ridiculously obvious, unless he was completely drunk or something.

Just as with many cultures in the Middle East today, however, women wore head-to-toe body veils/coverings, so that might account for the surprise the next day. Laban essentially quoted "the fine print" that Leah was first in line and that if Jacob wanted to have Rachel that it would cost him another seven years of labor. Needless to say Jacob grudgingly agreed to that part of the deal, making Laban a lot like a modern day corporate executive! Ironically, Leah ended up being the progenitor of King David—-and later, Jesus Christ Himself—-even though she was not the favored wife of Jacob.[2]

The Point:

Our values drive the decision-making processes that we use in real life every day; consequently, if you examine the actions of individuals, you can discover what they have chosen to value. Laban, described above, valued personal advantage over relationships and long-term cheap labor over family. Jacob was head over heels in love with Rachel, and that motivated him to marry her, as all his subsequent actions demonstrated.

His value, as with many of us, was connection, companionship, romantic love, and a desire to share his life with someone he cared deeply for. You and I face all sorts of choices every day and often face very complex and difficult decisions. Being human means that we have the ability to consciously and freely choose what truly matters, what is genuinely important, and what does not matter at all.

We literally have the freedom to choose anything we want to elevate in value; it can be brilliant and well thought out, or idiotic, stupid, and self-defeating. Sports fans certainly understand how finicky this can be; in the Seattle area, we have (and have had) several major-league sports franchises, some of which have performed rather poorly over the last several years.

Even in spite of disappointing seasons, die-hard fans still flock to the games, cheering and believing in their ability to win, if at least every once in a while. In the matter of values, belief comes first, choice comes second, and actions follow the values that we adopt.

Pilate called together the chief priests, the rulers and the people, and said to them, "You brought me this man as one who was inciting the people to rebellion. I have examined him in your presence and have found no basis for your charges against him. Neither has Herod, for he sent him back to us; as you can see, he has done nothing to deserve death. Therefore, I will punish him and then release him." With one voice they cried out, "Away with this man! Release Barabbas to us!" (Barabbas had been thrown into prison for an insurrection in the city, and for murder.) Wanting to release Jesus, Pilate appealed to them again... But with loud shouts they insistently demanded that he be crucified, and their shouts prevailed. So Pilate decided to grant their demand.

Luke 23:13–24 (NIV)

Background:

Jesus avoided all of the traps laid by His opponents, but essentially allowed Himself to be arrested and tried by the Jewish authorities at the end of His public ministry. He was tried and convicted by the Sanhedrin (the ruling council of the Jews located in Jerusalem), and sentenced to death, which they did not have the authority to carry out; the ruling government of the Roman Empire reserved the right to enforce capital punishment and did so frequently. As a result, the Jewish leaders sent Jesus to Pontius Pilate, the prefect (governor) of the region at the time.

Pilate was primarily military, and he was under instructions to maintain order among the territories assigned to him. He had already gotten off to a rocky start by allowing images of Caesar to be displayed in the city by soldiers, nearly creating a riot and widespread violence. Various accounts also describe Pilate's use of force, some violent, and others fatal, in dealing with the Jews, as well as a regular stream of complaints directed around him to superiors in Rome.

His own status of power was often shaky, and the fact that the Jews hated the Romans and disliked him in particular did not bode well for his military and political future. When the Jewish authorities brought Jesus to Pilate with a death sentence, he immediately wanted to get rid of the problem. In supporting biblical accounts, he first tried sending the problem to Herod, who was entertained but unwilling to deal with the issue.

After interrogating Jesus personally, Pilate knew right away that the entire set of criminal charges were unfounded and tried every trick in the book to dismiss them and free him. His last-ditch effort to end this politically thorny solution involved invoking a goodwill gesture, common during the Passover, in which a condemned prisoner in essence received a "get out of jail free" card, but that backfired when the crowd chose a convicted murderer instead. In the final analysis, Pilate chose to follow the "politically correct" path instead of the actually correct one.[3]

JOSEPH RINEHART & BRENDA RINEHART

The Point:

Every one of us faces pressures daily regarding our values, and consequently, our choices. Family members may ask us to prioritize our work demands around a child's sporting event. Employers may request extra hours away from home during peak periods or regarding critical business projects. Leisure events or vacation plans may get radically altered due to unrelated emergencies. Inevitably, we will face a collision between our own values or between our values and someone else's.

First, we realize that fact and accept it rather than get upset or try to cast blame. Second, we think about the actual values or issues involved and the degree of importance. One example might be an employer asking someone to work a particular Sunday; is the issue actually working on that particular day, or is it a matter of attending church that morning? Our older daughter, Jeanna, chooses to value attending church, not necessarily objecting to working the same day.

On certain weeks she attends the services just up the street, and then works her scheduled shift that same day, which equates to a win-win. Her younger sister, Naomi, feels more strongly about having the whole day set aside. Third, when necessary, make the right decision, not just the one that is easy. Keep in mind that in those situations where you need to stand firm, do so in a way that is agreeable as much as possible; too many times we can do what is right without doing it right!

84

Questions

VALUES SURVEY: Rank the following statements as follows:

    5 - Strongly agree with the statement
    4 - Agree with the statement
    3 - Neutral, neither agree nor disagree
    2 - Disagree with the statement
    1 - Strongly disagree with the statement

I.   I hate doing any task poorly, either at work or in my personal life.

II.   I love setting goals and enjoy reaching them.

III.   If I won the lottery tomorrow, I would never work again.

IV.   The United States is the greatest country in the world.

V.   I have a best friend that I talk to regularly.

VI.   I spend at least one hour a week talking with my family.

VII.   I attend church more than once a month.

VIII. People who live in this country need to speak English.

IX.   I like having the latest gadgets out on the market.

X.   I go out of my way to help other people.

XI.   I love learning new things every chance I get.

XII.   Stupid people annoy me greatly.

XIII.   I vote regularly when possible.

XIV.   I prefer to take chances that I am certain will work out.

XV.   My spouse/boyfriend/girlfriend and I talk at least three times a day.

General Values Key

XVI.   Excellence

XVII.   Degree of being driven

XVIII.   Work ethic

XIX.   Patriotism

XX.   Relationships

XXI.   Family

XXII.   Faith/religion

XXIII.   Tolerance of other cultures

XXIV.   Innovation

XXV.   Giving/serving

XXVI.   Learning/education

XXVII.   Tolerance

XXVIII.   Political involvement

XXIX.   Risk taking

XXX.   Companionship

** This is just a guide to help you start thinking about your personal values, it is not exhaustive or complete, nor are any answers good or bad. **

1. Think of a person you almost always disagree with. How do you typically react to them? What are your discussions like? Identify what values they represent that you do not agree with, and write them down.

2. List out the top five issues or topics you are *for*. What underlying personal value is tied to that? What about that really commands your attention, respect, and loyalty?

3. List out the top five issues or topics you are *against*. What underlying personal value is tied to that? What about that arouses strong feelings in you? Try to express that opposition in terms of a positive value; does that match with anything listed in the previous question?

4. List out ten one-word descriptions that you feel best describe you as a person. What personal values do these words represent? Do they match up at all with answers in the previous questions? Do any of them make you feel uncomfortable? Why or why not?

Prayer

LORD, thank you for creating me with the ability to choose what I stand for, believe in, and live by. I realize that many times I desire or value things that can create problems both for me and for those close to me; help me better understand the values that result in living the "full and abundant life" that you give me.

Guide me as I continue to understand what motivates my viewpoints and choices and to take the time to understand that in other people that I interact with every day. Most of all help me to live the values that you yourself stood for, taught, and modeled when you walked on the earth. Make me more like you every day. In Jesus's Name, Amen.

Red Rover, Red Rover: Cultural Values

There are three truths: my truth, your truth, and the truth.

Chinese Proverb

"Red rover, red rover, send Brenda right over!" I loved the sound of that simple phrase. I didn't realize it at the time, but I was hearing it so much because I was one of the smallest kids in my class. The kids on the opposing team knew that I didn't stand a chance of breaking through the band of their tightly held hands. They were great at keeping that part a secret. I just felt exhilarated, powerful, and included, so I ran toward them with all of my might, and when it was their turn to be called over, well, then my team would always pair me with the biggest kid in class. It didn't hurt that he was the cutest kid in class either. He held my hand as tight as he could, and although my fingers were surely purple from all of the attention I was getting, I held on tight...

— *Brenda*

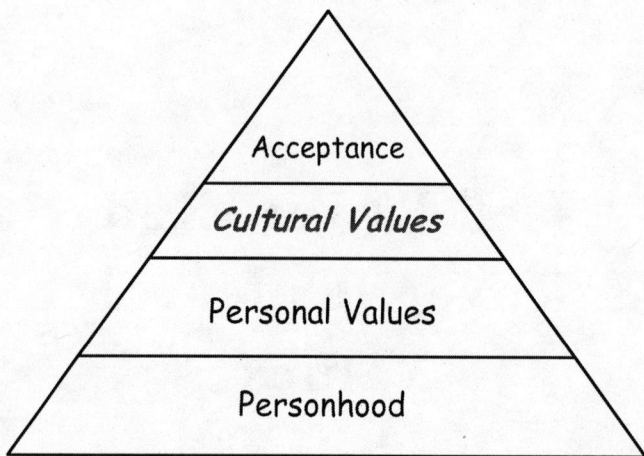

```
        /\
       /  \
      / Acceptance \
     /------------\
    / Cultural Values \
   /----------------\
  /  Personal Values  \
 /--------------------\
/     Personhood       \
```

As with most things in my life, my journey of faith is unusual and different than that of most other church-goers. I was born and raised Roman Catholic complete with eight years of parochial school, which makes sense given my Irish and Italian heritage. I was baptized as an infant, attended church fairly regularly, went through confirmation, observed communion, and went to confession. Upon reaching high school, I felt that something was missing and began doing research on other denominations to see if there was some "secret sauce" that would relieve the spiritual need that I felt.

After reading through Leo Rosten's *Religions of America* at my high school library, I chose what I thought was the "best fit" and let my fingers do the walking in the Yellow Pages. Once there, I selected a church and decided that I would try out the 8:30 a.m. service the next Sunday.

My only other experience with a Protestant church had been a hell-fire, pew-jumping, pastor-screaming Pentecostal church, so I was a little terrified about what to expect. Once there, I chose a seat at the very back and hoped that I would not be noticed until I was done "shopping." My invisibility plan was foiled when the fellow making the announcements asked if there were any visitors, and I reluctantly raised my hand and accepted the visitor packet from an usher.

I did not know any of the hymns; I felt out of place, and although I enjoyed the non-bellowing sermon (a pleasant surprise for me), the experience was a like a new pair of dress shoes—uncomfortable and slightly painful. After going for several weeks I got past that initial discomfort and decided to join the church, which literally required me to walk up in front of thousands of people to announce my decision.

While I am not a shy individual, I did not relish the experience of walking up in front of a crowd of people I did not know, and the ritual did not make much sense to me. I felt it was the "right thing to do," so I jumped through the hoops to get on-board and fit in with the rest of the people there. Anyone who has been to an evangelical church without growing up in that environment would probably shout an *amen*, proverbially speaking. Why did it feel so weird? Simply put, it was a different culture than what I had become accustomed to.

Culture is one of those words that has varied interpretations. The dictionary definition is, "patterns, traits, and products considered as the expression of a particular period, class, community, or population."[1] In other words, cultural values are the collective values and customs of a particular segment of society, such as Asian, American, European, and so forth. Anyone who has traveled to another country can attest to the difference in customs and behaviors.

Cultural values are an extension of personal values; while they may represent broadly held rules of behavior in a given social setting, they are still chosen by individuals. This broad set of accepted behaviors cannot exist without the collective adherence by those who claim to hold them. Since this may sound a little on the nebulous side, let's consider an analogy to help, especially with regard to the whole discussion of judgmental attitudes.

There were three basic religious groups of significance in Jesus's time, the Jews (both those native to Palestine and those living throughout the Roman Empire), the Gentiles (a general term for all of the non-Jewish nations), and the Samaritans (an interesting mix of both).

Each had distinctive cultural elements that uniquely identified them as well as contrasted them with one another; ironically, each also has a modern-day corollary that reflects modern cultural groups as well, particularly in the United States.

ONE WAY

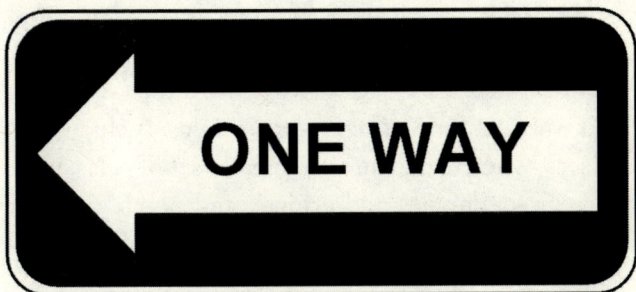

Historical Cultural Group: The Jews

As a group, the Jews enjoyed a long and spectacular religious history literally spanning thousands of years; most could trace their lineage back many generations to the time of the Patriarchs (Abraham, Isaac, and Jacob), and they had great pride in their heritage. In addition, they possessed an accurate, first-hand knowledge of God, as well as inspired Scriptures, which they regarded as the very words of Yahweh God and guarded strongly.

As a result, they lived by a strong moral code rooted in those writings, most notably including the Ten Commandments. The Jews practiced a number of religious rituals that included regular sacrifices, group worship at the temple in Jerusalem at regular intervals, and their own distinctive language.

From a personal standpoint, they also had specific customs regarding diet, dress, and so forth, as well as a tendency to interact rather exclusively with others of the same group. Probably due to their history, they tended to view non-Jews with a certain suspicion and distrust, with the exception of the Romans whom they openly despised.

At the extreme fringe were groups such as the Pharisees, who created an even greater set of rules, were rather closed-minded and critical, and notably one of the greatest opponents of Jesus Himself.[2]

Modern Corollary: Churched Christians

Christianity itself has a long history and is second only to Judaism in longevity among the three largest religions of the world; even the various denominations within Christianity have a heritage that spans centuries in some cases. Some families can trace their histories in the same faith or church over the course of multiple generations.

Most of these individuals gather regularly for worship, typically on Sunday morning, but often on Sunday evenings, Wednesday nights, and for other activities, such as the all too familiar potluck. For them, the Bible is clearly and indisputably the Word of God, and they readily and enthusiastically defend it with deep passion. Most adhere to a strong set of moral values and observe an entire set of rituals, some specifically religious (such as baptism), and others mixed with social implications (women's Bible studies, denominational programs, and the like).

Churched Christians also have a very well-defined inside language sometimes jokingly referred to as "Christianese," and it is peppered with terms such as *blessing, testimony, fellowship, sermon, scripture, prophecy*, and a myriad of others. Certain religious programs have a prominent role in their lives, such as Sunday school, Royal Rangers (an Assembly of God program), Woman's Missionary Union (Southern Baptist women's group), and AWANAS (the favorite kid's program of many independent evangelical churches).

At the extreme end, an entire litany of personal behavioral expectations is widely promulgated, shunning those who might "drink, smoke, dance, or go with girls that do." In addition, these individuals make a great deal of noise about specific social and political agendas, invoke the name of God for their particular candidates, and possess a very shrill tone about the personal and moral character of the rank and file "regular person" that may attend their church, teach their kids, or even live next door. While not everyone from this cultural group may represent this extreme, this is certainly the one most often caricatured or stereotyped in the minds of many American citizens.

Historical Cultural Group: The Gentiles

Another prominent cultural and religious group at the time of Jesus Christ was the Gentiles, namely anyone who did not have Jewish roots or religious faith. This included Greeks, Romans, Ethiopians, Athenians, Corinthians, and so on, and pretty much included those adhering to other religions or none altogether. As such, this group of people, unlike the Jews, did not possess a single unifying religious faith of any kind, but included a myriad of other religions that included the worship of idols or other physical representations of deity.

In terms of viable spiritual truth, the Gentiles were about as far from God, in concept and practice, that one could get; they had no knowledge of a single deity, and what they did claim to know was deemed incorrect or vastly different than the Jewish concepts. Worship typically included various ceremonies, including child sacrifice, ritual prostitution, wild religious feasts, and the like.

On the subject of morals, there was a staggering degree of variation, most often degenerating into a fairly well defined level of corruption that could not even resemble a set of moral standards; Roman culture stands as a fairly vivid example of this lifestyle and set of behaviors.

Unlike the Jews, Gentiles possessed a very uneven religious heritage and inconsistent spiritual history; consequently, cultural religious practices could become rather sporadic and, at times, irrelevant to their daily lives. Gentiles did not typically accept any religious writings as binding and authoritative and looked on groups such as the Jews as peculiar at best and at worst "strange and downright crazy," thus avoiding them.[3]

Modern Corollary: The Unchurched and/or Non-Religious

Even the most casual study of modern American culture reveals a vast diversity of belief systems and demonstrates little commitment to any single church or religious faith. Like the Gentiles of the ancient world at the time of Jesus, many do not believe in God at all, or hold a viewpoint very different than those who consider themselves religious in some form or fashion.

Of this particular cultural group, most do not attend church services regularly but might go at certain times of the year—typically Christmas, Mother's Day, and Easter. Most often, these individuals have a wide variety of moral standards and may not believe in God at all but prefer to refer to deity as a "higher power," "the Force" (of Star Wars fame), or some other nondescript terminology. As far as an actual faith, what they can accept as true regarding God is derived more from movies and television rather than exploration or religious study.

Due to the absence of core beliefs, many lead lives based on moral relativism. Many individuals in this cultural/religious category do not remotely understand the "churchgoing crowd" and find them intolerant, hypocritical, and sometimes "downright weird."

Historical Cultural Group: The Samaritans

One of the most visible religious groups during the time of Christ was the Samaritans. Ironically, many remember this particular faction more for the good samaritan that rescued an injured man on the road to Jericho than for their actual cultural heritage.

The Samaritan culture cropped up as a competing variant to the Jewish religion and lineage, formed more by ancient political expediency than personal conviction. From a historical standpoint, the Samaritans evolved from the survivors of the Assyrian deportation of the northern kingdom of Israel by King Shalmaneser I. King David's grandson, a monarch named Rehoboam, refused to give in to the requests and concessions of the northern tribes of the nation when he ascended to the throne, sparking a rebellion and civil war.

As a result, the kingdom created by David and Solomon split into two parts, a northern territory called Israel and a southern territory called Judah. Worship of Yahweh continued in Jerusalem at the Jewish temple, and Jeroboam, fearing the political consequences of a single religion, created idols, a rival priesthood, and a new religion in his own territory.

After several centuries, the northern kingdom of Israel succumbed to the rising political power of the nation of Assyria, and was deported into permanent captivity by the king at that time. As part of the strategy to prevent any resettlement by the original inhabitants, King Shalmaneser brought refugees from another region to permanently settle in the territory formerly belonging to Israel.

A problem developed, however, when wild lions began killing the new inhabitants, and due to religious superstitions, the Assyrians brought a Jewish priest in to teach the people about Yahweh.

Predictably, the new settlers simply added the Jewish deity to their own pantheon of gods and created a mixed religion that reflected neither Jewish sentiment nor native religious practice. As a result, the Jews regarded the Samaritans as possessing an impure ancestry, a corrupted religion, and altogether worthless; as a result, the Samaritans reciprocated with equal disgust toward them.[4]

Modern Corollary:
The Once-Churched

Many, though not all, of the populace of the United
States in the last century have had at least some brief
experience with a local church religious group of some
type or flavor. In my own experience as an ordained
minister, I have discovered that just about everyone has
attended some type of religious establishment as a child
or young adult and simply dropped out as they got older,
usually in their college years.

My own personal observations affirm that although
these individuals may have ceased attending church, they
clearly remember and value at least some of the experiences. For some, it might have been the style or type of
music (hymns), for others the type of public speaking
of the ministers (loud shouting or reflective contempla-
tion). Although they later "fell away" or shunned regular
church attendance, they still held on to specific aspects
of that experience and may even have sought it out later,
like when they got married or had children. Most would
accept the existence of God and at least some semblance
of core religious truth, though substantial variety exists
in the degree of that affirmation.

Morally speaking, these individuals have at least a
partial "moral compass" defined or shaped by their early
experiences; they may even readily accept religious writings such as the Bible but simply do not choose to live
by them. Their views regarding God often have some
degree of affinity as represented by established religious
thinking, but also end up clouded by alternative view-

points, usually represented by some aspect of popular culture.

Invariably, they can instantly recall the event or circumstances that resulted in their disenfranchisement from regular religious rituals, which may have centered on a particular pastor, church fight, or set of personalities at a certain church. Culturally they are neither irreligious—such as the purely unchurched—but neither are they the religious churched Christians. They remain suspended somewhat between the two extremes, much as the Samaritans of Jesus's own time.

To put it in the most unflattering and bluntest of terms, most religious conflicts occur more over cultural practices than actual theological truths. I would suspect that more churches have split over personalities and the color of the carpet in the auditorium than any substantive aspect of biblical truth.

Looking back in my own life, I can easily examine nearly all of the issues that evoked the most vehement responses at my church in Tennessee and find they reflected culture rather than hard-core spiritual principles. Let me clarify a few of them to illustrate the differences between what I felt was right and "what God told" those who sat on the other side of the proverbial table, philosophically speaking.

I thought delivering messages that brought the relevance of Jesus's teaching to everyday life would interest people; those in the core leadership felt that reminding people of the existence of hell and God's judgment on sin made more sense. In addition, I strongly disliked the idea of passing an offering plate, as it amounted to annoying people and asking for money; the leadership felt that it was "just the way God intended it."

Finally, I did not think it mattered what a person's background or spiritual pedigree was; the church leadership felt that those with a solid denominational background would be better members. Notice very clearly that *none* of those statements ever detracted from the deity of Jesus Christ, the accuracy of the Bible, the existence of God, or the nature of a genuine faith. In fact, one could easily argue that the controversies involved could never have been settled by quoting Bible verses or having any sort of theological debate; they represented *culture* not truth.

Going back to the discussion of personhood, humanity is first of all finite (limited in understanding, life span, and in every other way) as well as imperfect, whether you use the familiar terms of *fallen* or *sinful* or just prefer modern descriptions such as *messed up*, short-sighted or corrupt. The bottom line is that culture, no matter how ancient, well revered, or supposedly proven, is *manmade*; by nature of that fact it is suspect and arbitrary.

One of the reasons for checks and balances in business, politics, and economics is the simple fact that humanity has a history of flawed decision making. Clothing created by humans wears out and has to be replaced; systems of government and economics, even those such as democracy and capitalism, can end up filled with corruption and poor practices. In essence all manmade systems are filled with the same foibles,

MOVING FROM JUDGMENT

flawed thinking, and limitations associated with the rest of the human race.

God created men and women as the pinnacle of creation and possessing amazing abilities, but left to our own devices we can annihilate entire races, create weapons that can exterminate the entire planet several times over, and cheat our friends and family members out of what is rightfully theirs. Doesn't it make sense, then, that the same finite, limited, and sometimes corrupt human nature that arbitrarily created different cultures can be equally wrong and flawed as well?

This brings to mind the mathematical equation we introduced in the last chapter regarding our own values, of being composed both of those of the culture we have chosen, as well as the individual personal values we hold to:

$$V = V_p + V_c$$

Values   Personal   Cultural
Values   Values

As we look at the world, we look through rose-colored glasses of our own making. Granted, we exercise the God-given ability to freely choose those values, but we also practice the arrogance that our view of the world is, in fact, infallible and correct, and that everyone else is wrong; that attitude is precisely the same one as the judgmental Pharisees, modern churchgoers, and other philosophers of our day.

True acceptance and understanding, then, *must* be rooted in more than just surrendering one's own values or affirming someone else's. True acceptance, in fact, does not require either, as examined in the next chapter.

Going Deeper

Now he had to go through Samaria. So he came to a town in Samaria called Sychar, near the plot of ground Jacob had given to his son Joseph. Jacob's well was there, and Jesus, tired as he was from the journey, sat down by the well. It was about the sixth hour. When a Samaritan woman came to draw water, Jesus said to her, "Will you give me a drink?" (His disciples had gone into the town to buy food.) The Samaritan woman said to him, "You are a Jew and I am a Samaritan woman. How can you ask me for a drink?" (For Jews do not associate with Samaritans.) Jesus answered her, "If you knew the gift of God and who it is that asks you for a drink, you would have asked him and he would have given you living water." The woman said to him, "Sir, give me this water so that I won't get thirsty and have to keep coming here to draw water." He told her, "Go, call your husband and come back." "I have no husband," she replied. Jesus said to her, "You are right when you say you have no husband. The fact is, you have had five husbands, and the man you now have is not your husband. What you have just said is quite true." "Sir," the woman said, "I can see that you are a prophet. Our fathers worshiped on this mountain, but you Jews claim that the place where we must worship is in Jerusalem." Jesus declared, "Believe me, woman, a time is coming when you will worship the Father neither on this mountain nor in Jerusalem. You Samaritans worship what you do not know; we worship what we do know, for salvation is from the Jews. Yet a time is coming and has now come when the true worshipers will worship the Father in spirit and truth, for they are the kind of worshipers the Father seeks. God is spirit, and his worshipers must worship in spirit and in truth." The woman said, "I know that Messiah" (called Christ) "is coming. When he comes, he will explain everything to us." Then Jesus declared, "I who speak to you am he."

John 4:4–26 (NIV)

Background:

As mentioned previously, the Samaritans evolved from intermarriage between the survivors of the Assyrian deportation of the northern kingdom of Israel in 722 b.c. and the foreign groups transplanted in the same geography. When the southern kingdom of Judah returned from its own deportation by Babylon, the Samaritans offered to help rebuild the Jewish temple (Ezra 4:1–4) but were sternly denied; this marked the beginning of the distrust and intense dislike that existed between the Samaritans and mainstream Judaism.

Historically, the Jews preferred to take an entirely different and rather inconvenient, long travel route when going north, simply to avoid Samaria altogether. These historical snippets form the backdrop against which the account of Jesus interacting with the Samaritan woman took place.

The language here—Jesus *had* to go through Samaria—is significant since, as just mentioned, Jews took a long route just to avoid the place. Jesus sat at the well at what was more than likely the hottest part of the day, a time when no one in their right mind would be out and about, let alone someone drawing water.

The fact that the Samaritan woman chose that time of day implies that she made an effort to avoid the other women of the city, and given her living situation (five husbands and living unmarried to one at the time), she was probably a social outcast. When Jesus spoke to her, she was more shocked than surprised. To begin with, Jesus was Jewish and she was a Samaritan, two groups of people that literally hated one another. Second, Jesus was male and she was female, and a public conversation between genders was considered unacceptable.

Finally, her own living situation did not endear her to anyone, so initiating the conversation was three times over very surprising to her. As they chatted, Jesus managed to get her to reveal her existing living situation, and she immediately changed the subject from something personal to questions of religion. As with many aspects of the society, the Samaritans had a rival religion, complete with its own Bible (Genesis through Deuteronomy), place of worship, priests, and so on.

Her question centered on which group was really right, to which Jesus made several interesting responses. First, He pointed out, without being snide or arrogant, that the worship system of Samaria was not optimal, observed more by tradition than historical faith. Without breaking the flow of the conversation, Jesus made it clear that the question was largely irrelevant and that as the Messiah, that worship would not be focused on a location, but in a person.[5] Through it all, Jesus treated her with respect, courtesy, and good taste.

The Point:

Jesus conducted most of His ministry with Palestinian Jews, who—both by religion and culture—identified with the traditional worship of Yahweh of Israel. In addition, He traveled only within the borders of Israel, seldom moving into other areas; although, in this case He did so deliberately. Jesus had no issues engaging members of other cultures or backgrounds, as He interacted with a Roman centurion, Gentiles living in the country (Gadarene demoniac for example), and scores of others who sought Him out.

His encounter with the Samaritan woman illustrates how He easily engaged with someone with a very different background. Jesus focused first on the person, their wellbeing, and ultimately their spiritual welfare, not on side issues no matter how out of kilter they might have been.

In the same manner, as we encounter people whose background, language, and customs are unfamiliar, respect is always in order. His mission in talking with her was not persuading her to move to Jerusalem and convert to Judaism, but rather in dealing with the core issues of her relationship with God, namely Himself. Differences in culture do not always have the earmarks of differing nationalities, as numerous subcultures have evolved in the United States.

> Some men came down from Judea to Antioch and were teaching the brothers: "Unless you are circumcised, according to the custom taught by Moses, you cannot be saved." This brought Paul and Barnabas into sharp dispute and debate with them. So Paul and Barnabas were appointed, along with some other believers, to go up to Jerusalem to see the apostles and elders about this question... Then some of the believers who belonged to the party of the Pharisees stood up and said, "The Gentiles must be circumcised and required to obey the law of Moses." The apostles and elders met to consider this question. After much discussion, Peter got up and addressed them: "Brothers, you know that some time ago God made a choice among you that the Gentiles might hear from my lips the message of the gospel and believe. God, who knows the heart, showed that he accepted them by giving the Holy Spirit to them, just as he did to us. He made no distinction between us and them, for he purified their hearts by faith. Now then, why do you try to test God by putting on the necks of the disciples a yoke that neither we nor our fathers have been able to bear? No! We believe it is through the grace of our Lord Jesus that we are saved, just as

they are."... When they finished, James spoke up: "Brothers, listen to me. Simon has described to us how God at first showed his concern by taking from the Gentiles a people for himself... It is my judgment, therefore, that we should not make it difficult for the Gentiles who are turning to God. Instead we should write to them, telling them to abstain from food polluted by idols, from sexual immorality, from the meat of strangled animals and from blood. For Moses has been preached in every city from the earliest times and is read in the synagogues on every Sabbath."

Acts 15:1–21 (NIV)

Background:

As previously mentioned, the early followers of Christ came from the community in which He lived, namely, Palestinian Judaism. All of the twelve disciples that formed His leadership team had direct roots in the various territories of Israel and naturally the church in Jerusalem was Jewish in nature. As early Christianity moved throughout the territories of the Roman Empire, however, the introduction of Gentiles (non-Jews) changed the ethnicity, and consequently the culture, that had been associated with it.

In the opening chapters of the book of Acts, many of the early believers still went to the Temple in Jerusalem to worship, and even Paul would speak in the synagogues of the cities he traveled to. Some of the Jewish

Christian believers felt strongly that these "newer arrivals" needed to observe the important aspects of Judaism, including the rite of circumcision, dietary laws, and traditions of the faith; in other words, they needed to convert to Judaism while still maintaining their faith in Jesus Christ.

As with many issues, this probably had been bubbling under the surface for a while before reaching a crisis point; as a result the leadership of the entire Christian faith met in Jerusalem to come to grips with the question. Paul, as both a theologian and missionary to the Gentiles, had strong feelings on the subject, and his thoughts are captured in a number of the books he wrote, such as Galatians.

Peter also had dealt with Cornelius, a Roman soldier, who came to faith in Jesus and shared the experience at the conference. James, the same writer of the book in the New Testament, one of the leaders of the Jerusalem church, cited Old Testament support for the issue as well. In the final decision, the consensus of the leadership was that Gentiles did not have to adopt Jewish customs or practices in order to legitimately be part of the faith. In essence, the more cultural aspects of the early faith were declared unnecessary to having a genuine relationship with Christ.[6]

The Point:

Often we can get rather attached and enthusiastic about things we enjoy or feel comfortable with. For example, when I was pastor of the church in Tennessee, one of the members insisted that the Bible only spoke about hymns when referring to music in the services. What is ironic is that the music she was referring to had been written over one thousand years after the verses she quoted.

Another example is the church government of many denominations reflects American democracy more than the structures described in the writings of the New Testament. Biblical truth deals with essential issues of life on planet Earth, how to live out a viable faith, and addresses many issues but also remains silent on a number of others. Forcing a particular set of cultural preferences on another group of people on areas the Bible doesn't even speak on typically creates chaos and resentment.

Churches in Africa do not have to sing in English, nor do congregations in South America have to listen to sermons in Swahili. Obviously, every culture has strengths and weaknesses, and all have aspects that contradict revealed truth, but one is not better than any other; usually it just happens to be more familiar.

> While Paul was waiting for them in Athens, he was greatly distressed to see that the city was full of idols. So he reasoned in the synagogue with the Jews and the God-fearing Greeks, as well as in the marketplace day by day with those who happened to be there. A group of Epicurean and Stoic philosophers began to dispute with him. Some of them asked, "What is this babbler trying to say?" Others remarked, "He seems to be advocating foreign gods." They said this because Paul was preaching the good news about Jesus and the resurrection.

Then they took him and brought him to a meeting of the Areopagus, where they said to him, "May we know what this new teaching is that you are presenting? You are bringing some strange ideas to our ears, and we want to know what they mean." (All the Athenians and the foreigners who lived there spent their time doing nothing but talking about and listening to the latest ideas.) Paul then stood up in the meeting of the Areopagus and said: "Men of Athens! I see that in every way you are very religious. For as I walked around and looked carefully at your objects of worship, I even found an altar with this inscription: *To An Unknown God.* Now what you worship as something unknown I am going to proclaim to you. "The God who made the world and everything in it is the LORD of heaven and earth and does not live in temples built by hands ... we should not think that the divine being is like gold or silver or stone—an image made by man's design and skill. In the past God overlooked such ignorance, but now he commands all people everywhere to repent. For he has set a day when he will judge the world with justice by the man he has appointed. He has given proof of this to all men by raising him from the dead." When they heard about the resurrection of the dead, some of them sneered, but others said, "We want to hear you again on this subject." At that, Paul left the Council.

Acts 17:16–33 (NIV)

Background:

Paul had an incredible academic background and spoke several languages fluently; both his writing as well as his recorded speaking shows remarkable ability and a wide range of knowledge. Since he grew up outside Israel, he possessed a great familiarity of the Greek and Roman cultural fabric, which dominated the world in his day. Paul's training in Judaism, along with his education in general, outfitted him perfectly for the mission of taking the Christian faith through the territories of Rome.

Possessing citizenship as a Roman opened many additional doors to his efforts. One particularly striking ability that Paul used both well and often was to engage the local culture to communicate the message of Jesus Christ. In 1 Corinthians 9:2, Paul writes, "I become all things to all people, in order that I might win some."

As Paul arrived at the city of Athens, the birthplace of democracy and philosophy, he sought out an audience at the intellectual center of the city. Because the Athenians wanted to make certain that they had appeased every possible deity that existed, they had erected an altar and temple "to the unknown god" not referring to a specific one but as a type of "wild card."

Since everyone listening to him would have been familiar with the altar, Paul chose to use it as a starting point for discussing the teachings of Christ. During his speech, Paul also quoted their own literature as a means of capturing their attention and engaging them in considering his message. When all was said and done, as happened often, some believed and others did not, but his approach did have an impact.[7]

The Point:

Paul did not actually believe that the altar had been erected to worship either Yahweh or Jesus Christ, but he used it as a great starting point for presenting to a skeptical audience. Paul used every cultural tool at his disposal for the simple purpose of communicating the faith to people with no background to grasp it. When speaking to Jews in a local synagogue, he had a solid foundation to begin explaining things.

Jews accepted the Old Testament as the revealed word from Yahweh. They believed in God deeply and expected the coming of the Messiah. Gentiles typically worshiped many deities, engaged in wild religious practices, and had no concept of authoritative religious writings.

Paul communicated in ways that his audience could readily understand and relate to, and used various opportunities that cultures gave him when communicating that. He used the "altar to the known god" in Athens and no doubt many other examples, as evidenced in the writings that are now a part of the New Testament.

Truth does indeed matter, but culture is often neutral; when Biblical truth and culture collide, God's Word prevails. Much of the "Christian culture" that has evolved over the years in the United States is not an issue of truth as much as institutions and practices that had wide acceptance at one time.

The practice of Sunday schools, hymns, the length and style of services, are not mandated by God but cultural aspects that are not in and of themselves sacred. Keeping that in mind can help all of us to better address not only those outside Christianity but also in engage people that have vastly different cultural backgrounds.

Questions

1. Describe some traditions that your family practiced while you were growing up. When telling someone outside your family about them, what kinds of reactions have you observed? What was the most negative one? How did you feel listening to that? What lessons from that experience can you apply when dealing with unfamiliar customs or cultural practices?

2. How often do you interact with individuals from other nationalities? Does that cause you any discomfort? Why or why not? Specifically, which nationalities, cultures, or languages did they represent? Do you have a group you feel the most comfortable with? Why or why not?

3. Have you traveled either internationally or to an area where the majority of the residents were from a different culture (Native American reservation, missions trip, China Town in San Francisco, etc.)? Did you find any commonality between your own background and experiences and that group?

4. Do you speak any foreign languages (Russian, Japanese, French, Italian, German, etc.)? If yes, how did that affect your understanding of the nation or people? If not, what familiarity do you have with the customs and practices of a different culture?

5. Have you ever had the experience of trying to communicate with a person, either personally or profes-

sionally, who did not speak your language well/at all, and whose language you did not speak well/at all? How did you manage to get ideas across to the other person? What about that experience can help you with communication in general?

Prayer

LORD, you created the human race to express itself in a wide variety of ways throughout history and in today's times in nations throughout the world. While I may not always understand or completely appreciate the aspects of unfamiliar cultures, help me see that variety as a positive thing. Give me insight into your truth that transcends any and all cultures, including the one that I am a part of. Guide my thinking to look at the world with *you* at the center instead of myself, to accept truth in "different wrappers" that still follows the principles of Your written word.

Keep my life concentrated on truth, not fear or pride, especially when dealing with something that is new or different. Most of all, help my words, attitudes, and actions to reveal Your grace, mercy, and love to anyone that I come across, no matter what background they may come from. Help me view myself as a citizen of heaven and treat others in a way that brings You honor, praise, and glory. In Jesus's Name, Amen.

Truth or Dare: Acceptance

To love another person is to see the face of God.

Les Miserables

My little brother, like most younger siblings, wanted more than anything to one up me—to know something that I didn't, to be better than me at anything, or just have something better than I did. This simple reality made Truth or Dare the ultimate game for him, and he wanted to play all the time. He couldn't really lose because either way he could challenge me. My choices were to tell something or complete the dare, which with my brother meant certain death, so I always skipped that part. The problem was that Truth or Dare was anything but truthful, because to impress and be accepted you had to one up the other player(s).

The more grandiose the tale the more likely it would be met with skepticism, but the little lies, well, they were tough. Maybe he really did eat four roly-poly bugs off the sidewalk, and if he did, well, "How gross was that?" Pretty soon everyone at school would be talking and the tale would spread and the other kids just might think he was pretty brave ...

— *Brenda*

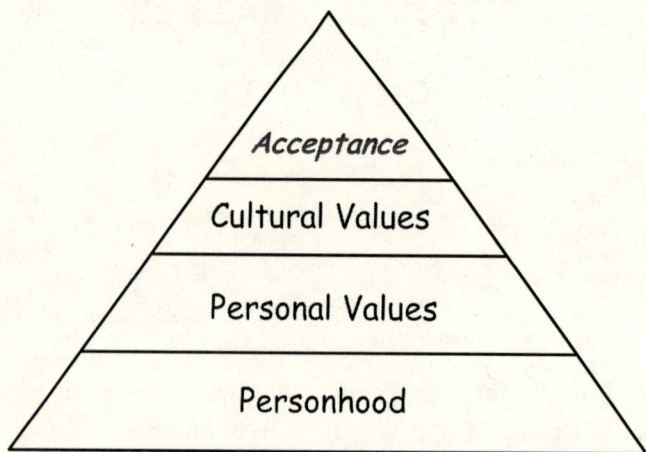

Now we get down to "where the rubber meets the road" so to speak, with regard to judgmental attitudes, viewpoints, and behaviors. Admittedly, once you have had an unpleasant encounter in this regard, it's a lot like drinking prune juice, castor oil, or some other detestable remedy associated with childhood. Not only can you vividly recall the revolting taste but often all of the negative emotions associated with the experience.

The experience I briefly related at the beginning of the book has an amazing amount of venom, pain, anger, and angst associated with it that would be a book all by itself. I swore that one day I would create a quasi-fictional story with fabricated names that revealed the "untold story" squelched by the victors in that conflict.

In all reality, the principles contained in this very volume came not from some dream, nighttime revelation, or profound thought process, but out of the years spent associated with trying to sort all of that out. As a young pastor, I had assumed that most situations could reach positive resolution by open discussion, compromise, and some type of meeting of the minds; in reality that proved to be both naïve and self-defeating.

Having an optimistic viewpoint on life frequently can position you as a positive person and someone that others look to for encouragement. The down side of that worldview, however, can also result in either assuming that things will always turn out rosy or in failing to accurately account for the reality of human behavior. I have a saying that I made my own: The difference between being jaded and street smart is a matter of degree.

A truly jaded person lives a pessimistic and almost paranoid existence in which every other person simply wants to take advantage of them. You undoubtedly have met people like this; they assume that the sky is falling and that everyone is out to get them. An individual with a street-smart mentality assumes that things can certainly be just fine but stops long enough to ask those offering a favor the simple question of, "Why do you want to be nice to me?"

In the world of business and personal relationships, one can gain both understanding and benefit by understanding opposite points of view, finding common ground, and establishing compromise in which each party feels they have gained something meaningful.

In battles over personal or cultural values, this approach seldom works effectively. Relating this to my own experience in this regard, I held the assumption that just understanding the issues and giving some ground would rectify the increasingly strident tone of the conflict among the church leadership.

The more traditional folks requested that we set up a committee system to balance some of the power throughout the church membership. This seemed like a reasonable request until the group chosen to do that was entirely of their particular mindset. The longer the conflict went on, the more I gradually tried to give up for the sake of a peaceful congregation. This became difficult when I began to get pointed questions from the majority of the people in the church as to why the things they loved were changing. Most of them did not have a church background, so it didn't make sense to them.

When all was said and done, in fact, none of the compromises or "middle ground" mattered because the goal was making the church fit a very specific culture, and that was chosen by the people in power. These kinds of ideological wars most often produce losers on both sides and create the propagation of judgmental attitudes. The actual reason for these kinds of situations actually has to do with the way people view the whole concept of acceptance.

Human nature dictates that one individual will naturally seek out others that are most like them; those who listen to rock tend to hang out with rockers; skateboarders prefer the company of others who skateboard; and churchgoing people tend to gravitate to those that believe and live the way that they do.

None of this is inherently wrong. Most of us feel some sort of bond or commonality when we come across another person with either similar viewpoints or sets of experiences. In the grand scheme of vales we basically look at affinity or acceptance using the following equation:

$$V_{(1)} = V_{(2)}$$

My Values   Your Values

Admittedly, given the nature of human beings, not a singular set of values will completely equal that of another person, ever. Even very close relationships, such as a happily married couple, seldom match exactly. If you don't believe it, try having a discussion with someone close to you that feels you do not accept them—in most cases it will boil down to your affirmation (or lack of it) regarding their lifestyle, choices, position on some issue, or something similar.

In the flawed, imperfect human psyche, acceptance equates to some form of personal endorsement, usually tied to some set of thoughts, philosophies, beliefs, or behaviors. For example, when I was first making my journey of faith, my mother flatly refused to give any credence to it, saying something to the effect that I had "become one of those Babdists" (purposely mispronounced).

Jesus drew people to Himself literally by the thousands; some came searching for truth, others wanted to see or personally experience the supernatural miracles, and still others were just curious—each part of the crowd that followed Him had different reasons for doing so. The religious establishment of that time, populated mainly by the Pharisees—a very strict, conservative religious group—and the Sadducees—a more liberal sect that dominated the priesthood—did a better job of driving people away.

These leaders certainly equated the right values and behavior with having the favor and acceptance of God and spiritual health. At this point Jesus and these religious leaders clashed, because He operated on an entirely different wavelength that offended them.

One of the best portraits of the concept of acceptance occurs in the middle of one of these conflicts, as told in John, chapter 8, as follows:

> At dawn he appeared again in the temple courts, where all the people gathered around him, and he sat down to teach them. The teachers of the law and the Pharisees brought in a woman caught in adultery. They made her stand before the group and said to Jesus, "Teacher, this woman was caught in the act of adultery. In the Law Moses commanded us to stone such women. Now what do you say?" They were using this question as a trap, in order to have a basis for accusing him."
>
> John 8:2–6 (NIV)

Jesus came once again to the Jewish temple in Jerusalem, the main gathering point for Jews making sacrifices and offering prayers to Yahweh—it was literally the nerve center of religious life and ceremony. Right there, in front of the crowd that had gathered, the Pharisees threw a woman down in front of Him, claiming they had caught her in adultery and, according to Jewish custom, would have already had several witnesses ready to testify.

At this point they reminded Jesus that the Torah (the books of Genesis through Deuteronomy) identified the act as a clear violation of the law, God's written word, and that Moses himself had mandated death by execution.

Keep in mind that at this point the Pharisees had less interest in real justice, but rather had created a no-win scenario for Jesus in front of a large group of people. On the one hand, if He stayed consistent with His teachings and just said to let her go, then He contradicted the very essence of the Jewish religion and would certainly be brought to the authorities.

At the other end of the spectrum, Jesus could agree with them, condemning the woman to death, which would then discredit Him and His teachings in front of a large number of followers. He clearly tried to ignore them, but the Pharisees pressed Him to respond to the situation at hand. Jesus responded with, "If any one of you is without sin, let him be the first to throw a stone at her."

Jesus neither agreed nor disagreed with their position, but in fact expertly turned the tables on the entire situation and put the burden back on the Pharisees—they could take on the arrogance of being sinless or just give up and walk away, which is what they ended up doing. Ironically, those who were older and wiser left first, but when all was said and done, just Jesus and the accused woman stood in the Temple. His final words to her capture the essence of acceptance:

> At this, those who heard began to go away one at a time, the older ones first, until only Jesus was left, with the woman still standing there. Jesus straightened up and asked her, "Woman, where are they? Has no one condemned you?" "No one, sir," she said. "Then neither do I condemn you," Jesus declared. "Go now and leave your life of sin."
>
> John 8:9–11

Jesus had the right, both by His deity as well as the written laws of Moses, to legitimately condemn the woman for her actions, but instead, He chose not to; He exercised mercy. In other words, He accepted her, even though the religious crowd did just the opposite. Jesus appealed to the outcasts, the disenfranchised, the ones that the leaders of the day considered unworthy.[1]

In this and many other similar instances, He met her where she was, affirmed her value as a being created by God, and gave her real acceptance. Notice, however, another critical detail in the account—Jesus didn't affirm or condone the act of adultery, or even of whatever lifestyle she had been involved in up to that point. Instead, He urged her to leave that life behind, to change, and begin making better choices.

JOSEPH RINEHART & BRENDA RINEHART

126

Rather than concentrating on her values, Jesus instead accepted her personhood as a being created by God and having infinite personal worth—sound familiar? Looking at the whole issue this way, then, the whole equation of values realistically looks this way:

$$V_{(1)} \neq V_{(2)}$$

My Values   Your Values

As stated previously, equal values rarely exist. As individuals with an independent sense of self we can choose values that statistically will not completely line up with those that someone else may select. In addition, many people consider *acceptance of a person with differing values* as creating the need to compromise or surrender some aspect of their own values. The equation, similar to what we have looked at before, would be expressed as:

$$V_{(1)} - X = V_{(2)}$$

My Values   Your Values

In this context, X represents some value, aspect, viewpoint, etc., that needs to be removed from the values from one person to accept the values of the other person. In the entire science of relationships, meeting in the middle—usually termed compromise—represents the best possible outcome in the event of disagreement or conflict.

Dysfunctional relationships, by contrast, typically involve one person always winning and the other always giving in. Make no mistake, in relationships the best operational procedure ends up involving each side giving up something in order to reach a sensible middle ground.

In the whole matter of personal acceptance and the question of values, if the principles involved represent something lower in the hierarchy of values, then acceptance in that realm is relatively simple. If the value is one at the core of an individual's value system (remember the "Supreme Court" analogy?), then at this point *compromise* is not a good word but rather a "dirty word."

In the minds of most churched Christians, for example, this represents a slippery slope that can result in personal difficulty and spiritual corruption. In the extreme sense, some churchgoers will cite passages about the teaching of separation, which basically means not taking on the value system of the society about them, usually called "the world" or "worldly things." Matthew Henry's Commentary on 2 Corinthians 6:11–18 spelled this out in no uncertain terms, as follows:

> The caution also extends to common conversation. We should not join in friendship and acquaintance with wicked men and unbelievers. Though we cannot wholly avoid seeing and hearing, and being with such, yet we should never choose them for

friends. We must not defile ourselves by converse with those who defile themselves with sin.[2]

In this commentary, the viewpoint shared is that the best policy is to stay away from anyone whose lifestyle differs from what someone perceived as the correct biblical lifestyle. The danger in doing so, according to that viewpoint, is becoming the "frog in the kettle" in which someone becomes desensitized to corrupt influences and ends up just "joining in." The life and character of Jesus, however, demonstrated the opposite—His opponents criticized Him for dining with and "hanging out" with sinners and tax collectors as friends.

Acceptance cannot rest in some attempt to equalize value systems between human beings. Since Jesus walked the earth as fully divine and fully human, and still managed to accept people, the answer has to be somewhere else. This takes us back to the story of the woman caught in adultery, as well as the point at which God created the human race—Personhood.

The entire preceding discussion grew out of one specific element of personhood, namely self-determination, the ability to freely make choices. Personhood certainly creates the capability of constructing the choices that result in an individual's value system, but transcends it entirely as well. The equations presented previously demonstrated the impossibility of having identical value systems, but the intrinsic value of personhood paints an entirely different, but highly relevant, picture:

$$P_{(1)} = P_{(2)}$$

My Personhood   Your Personhood

Explained another way, the intrinsic value of individual human beings also breaks out in the following manner, echoing once again the well-known phrase that "all men are created equal":

MY VALUE	=	YOUR VALUE
PERSONHOOD		*PERSONHOOD*
Created in God's Image		Created in God's Image
Christ Died For		Christ Died For
Recipient of God's Love		Recipient of God's Love

Personhood indicates the inherent value that human beings possess by virtue of creation by God Himself; you may recall that human life was regarded as something immensely valued through the writings of the Old Testament with direct references to the "image of God" in humans. Furthermore, the writings of the New Testament make the case over and over that Christ died for the members of the human race, individually and collectively. Paul, who once fought against Christianity, wrote the following words in this regard, in Romans 5:7–8:

> Very rarely will anyone die for a righteous man, though for a good man someone might possibly

dare to die. But God demonstrates his own love for us in this: While we were still sinners, Christ died for us.

Looking at this principle, the death of Christ was for all human beings, demonstrating the immense value God places on us, but also made equal opportunity available to *all* people as well. The facts apply whether or not a person chooses to act on what has been made available; note the phrase "while we were still sinners." This means that God had and has immense love for the people He created, and that all stand before Him as loved equally.

Granted, those who have chosen a relationship with Him enjoy the forgiveness that comes through Christ and the benefits of actively experiencing that love, but the depth and breadth of that love exists for all. Simply put, Jesus Christ accepted very flawed, imperfect human beings based on their personhood, not their values, lifestyle, or any aspect of their behavior.

Clearly He taught both the value of love as well as following the principles contained in His teachings; in doing so He did not condone or approve of choices made outside of those principles, which Jesus clearly referred to when he stated, "Go and sin no more"; this was a phrase heard often by those that encountered Him.

Acceptance does not require the compromise of your personal values or the embracing of someone else's position, lifestyle, or values. In mathematical terms, our value system (personally chosen values plus adopted cultural values) will never equal that of another person exactly. Trying to reconcile the two through compromise seldom brings satisfaction. True acceptance of another person instead relies on the values derived from creation by God, the death of Christ, and His love toward every individual person.

Viewed this way, all humans possess equal value that has nothing to with work, personality, attractiveness, values, behaviors, or anything else. Acceptance simply recognizes that all humans have equal value and treat one another with the dignity and respect due that position in the order of creation.

Going Deeper

The king of Jericho was told, "Look! Some of the Israelites have come here tonight to spy out the land." So the king of Jericho sent this message to Rahab: "Bring out the men who came to you and entered your house, because they have come to spy out the whole land." But the woman had taken the two men and hidden them. She said, "Yes, the men came to me, but I did not know where they had come from. At dusk, when it was time to close the city gate, they left. I don't know which way they went. Go after them quickly. You may catch up with them." ... [Rahab] said to them, "I know that the LORD has given this land to you and that a great fear of you has fallen on us, so that all who live in this country are melting in fear because of you. We have heard how the LORD dried up the water of the Red Sea for you when you came out of Egypt, and what you did to Sihon and Og, the two kings of the

Amorites east of the Jordan, whom you completely destroyed. When we heard of it, our hearts melted in fear and everyone's courage failed because of you, for the LORD your God is God in heaven above and on the earth below."

Joshua 2:2–5, 9–11 (NIV)

Salmon the father of Boaz, whose mother was Rahab, Boaz the father of Obed, whose mother was Ruth, Obed the father of Jesse.

Matthew 1:5 (NIV)

By faith the prostitute Rahab, because she welcomed the spies, was not killed with those who were disobedient.

Hebrews 11:31 (NIV)

In the same way, was not even Rahab the prostitute considered righteous for what she did when she gave lodging to the spies and sent them off in a different direction?

James 2:25 (NIV)

Background:

Moses led the nation of Israel out of Egypt, leaving their life of slavery behind and looking toward a new home in what was referred to as the promised land. After two to three years of travel on foot, with livestock, the estimated two and a half million people blew the chance to settle in Palestine and ended up wandering essentially in circles for another thirty-seven years.

Because of his own disobedience in striking the rock instead of speaking to it, Moses himself did not enter the land, though he did get to see it from a distance before dying on Mount Nebo. Joshua remembered the fiasco of sending out spies into the area publicly (that was part of the reason for the whole forty years of wandering), and thus enlisted two men to go on a "covert mission."

Their task was to size up the defenses of the city of Jericho, a strategic, highly fortified location that stood between the nation and the rest of the territory. Presumably, the two men had some type of military experience and may have even served under Joshua who had been the general of the army under Moses.

To keep a low profile, the two men stayed at a brothel, not to engage in any "extracurricular activities" so to speak, but rather because it was the kind of place where people would come and go and not ask any questions. Their clever approach did not work, however, and the city authorities were soon banging at the door of Rahab's place of business, demanding she turn them over to them at once. Rather than engage in an elaborate lie, she admitted that they had stayed at her residence, but feigned any knowledge of their identities or true intentions, and then sent the police force on a wild goose chase in the wrong direction.

Once the threat was gone, Rahab went up to the rooftop where the men had hidden, clearly declared her faith in Yahweh, and asked for mercy when the Israelite army stormed the city in the not so distant future. Jericho and Israel were nation-states at war, so Rahab took a substantial risk in "aiding and abetting" a clear enemy, and, conversely, the two spies essentially spared her and her family in a clear act of mercy.

Later, when the city fell, they stood by their commitment, even though her personal and spiritual record was not the most flattering. Tradition says that one of the spies was Salmon and that he and Rahab married, which is a significant turnaround from her prior life.

Factually speaking, however, the biblical record places her as directly in the line of King David, and ultimately, in the line of Jesus Christ Himself. James and the writer of Hebrews hail Rahab not as a "woman of the evening" but rather a tremendous example of faith and obedience in the most challenging of circumstances. The two spies specifically treated her as a friend rather than an enemy, praised what she did right without condoning what she may have done wrong, and looked at her in light of her future rather than her past.[3]

The Point:

If you interviewed most people on the street today, most would perceive "women of the evening" in a less than positive light.[4] In some ways, just the way Israel would have in ancient times. Many times it seems like human nature immediately gravitates toward assuming the worst about the people. Granted, there are individuals that seem to ooze dissatisfaction, discomfort, and negativity. In those cases it may be hard to look past their personality.

Our greatest gift to someone is to accept them for who they are and where they are, which does not mean that we have to give approval or somehow condone things that go against our personal and cultural values.

First, we should look at people from the point of their personhood—made in the image of God, valuable to Him, and someone He loved so much to send His only son to die for. It isn't about worthiness, because if we applied the same standard to ourselves, none of us would make the grade either. Looking past the surface to the real person inside can also make a profound difference, since few people get to travel through life without others criticizing them.

The three steps outlined in the interactions with Rahab also serve as great ways to interact with others. To begin with, treat them as a friend rather than an enemy. No one likes rejection, judgment, or criticism, whether warranted or not, and if you polled most of the population they have probably experienced it far more than they wanted to.

Dare to be different, to reach out to someone based on the love of Jesus Christ, and to demonstrate it rather than just talk about it. Instead of seeing casual encounters in your day-to-day life as coincidental or unimportant, treat them as appointments from God to make an impact in the lives of others. Granted, some days will be unusually challenging, but the rewards are far greater than you could possibly imagine.

Second, praise the things they do or may be doing that are positive, without condoning choices or actions that you may not agree with. As we mentioned before, affirming and accepting someone does not require giving your stamp of approval or affirmation with things you do not agree with. Concentrate on what you can say something positive about, and, if possible, something that resonates with your own values. Encouragement is always much more welcome than criticism.

Finally, look at them in light of their future potential. I would bet that if those men had gotten a glimpse into the future and seen Rahab as one of the ancestors of their greatest king as well as of the Messiah, it would have blown their minds! The fact is that no one just emerges into great accomplishments or character by fiat; it takes place over time and with opportunity.

In his very early years, Billy Graham, one of the greatest spiritual leaders of our time, was invited to a tent meeting to hear an evangelist, and was unable to find a seat. The usher, whose name and identity still are unknown, put a few chairs in the choir loft for Graham and his friends to sit. That very simple act of kindness paved the way for one of the greatest men of God to start down the right path.[5]

> But if you are led by the Spirit, you are not under law. The acts of the sinful nature are obvious: sexual immorality, impurity and debauchery; idolatry and witchcraft; hatred, discord, jealousy, fits

of rage, selfish ambition, dissensions, factions and envy; drunkenness, orgies, and the like. I warn you, as I did before, that those who live like this will not inherit the kingdom of God. But the fruit of the Spirit is love, joy, peace, patience, kindness, goodness, faithfulness, gentleness and self-control. Against such things there is no law.

Galatians 5:16–23 (NIV)

Background:

Galatia was not a city but a region in Asia Minor, or modern-day Turkey; Paul had traveled extensively throughout the area and planted churches, as recorded in the book of Acts. As mentioned in the previous chapter, as Christianity (termed "the Way" in Roman times) gained greater adoption among the Gentile community, some of the more traditional Jewish believers began to feel uncomfortable about the seeming loss of emphasis on the culture they were most familiar with. While the gathering of the entire leadership in Jerusalem eventually settled the matter, controversy ended up brewing regarding the issue.

Paul wrote the book of Galatians to combat the notion that followers of Jesus Christ had to adopt Jewish customs and practices, including observance of the rite of circumcision and following the Old Testament laws. Throughout the book he deals with the issue in some detail, making the clear case that faith in Christ alone brought about acceptance with God and that no human effort could supersede the death of Christ in reconciling man to God. This particular section of the book focuses more on the application of these truths to the everyday life of the follower of Christ.

Paul presents the simple facts that since the human race fell, that left to their own devices they would end up getting into mischief, making poor choices, and creating moral and spiritual chaos in their own lives—termed the "sinful nature." Once a person enters into a relationship with God through Jesus Christ, the Holy Spirit creates a new nature within a human being, allowing them to choose a better way of living, and that life manifests itself openly in the terms such as *love*, *joy*, *peace*, *patience*, *kindness*, *gentleness*, and so forth. Naturally, when an individual consistently follows the type of life honoring to Jesus, these words should describe their character, demeanor, and actions.[6]

The Point:

Even the most casual observation of the human race paints a picture that every one of us is imperfect even on our best days. If you ever enjoy "people watching," go to a park, mall, or other well-attended location, and take an hour just in surveillance mode; take note of the behaviors and interactions that you observe. People of all shapes and sizes, walks of life, backgrounds, and styles of dress will display a myriad of actions—some cruising, others bored, some arguing, and such. In the lives of the followers of Jesus, there should be a demonstrable difference that can be observed.

Some of the most difficult, obnoxious, mean, and dysfunctional people I have ever met claim to have a close relationship with Christ. According to Paul, our lives should reveal the character, values, and actions that Jesus Himself would have if walking on the earth today. That does not require us to stop thinking, annihilate our personalities, or turn into an army of clones (thank you, George Lucas!).

It does, however, reinforce the simple fact that our lives should shine rather than annoy, judge, or intimidate. We can still hold to our values and personal preferences, but our way of relating to others does not require some kind of rude arrogance to somehow prove we have the best opinion. When we act that way, our lives reflect much more the "works of the flesh" as Paul describes it than the "fruit of the Spirit."

> With what shall I come before the LORD and bow down before the exalted God? Shall I come before him with burnt offerings, with calves a year old? Will the LORD be pleased with thousands of rams, with ten thousand rivers of oil? Shall I offer my firstborn for my transgression, the fruit of my body for the sin of my soul? He has showed you, O man, what is good. And what does the LORD require of you? *To act justly and to love mercy and to walk humbly with your God.*
>
> Micah 6:6–8 (NIV)

Background:

After the death of Solomon, the kingdom established and grown by David split into two parts: a northern section, Israel, headed by various dynasties, and a southern section, Judah, ruled by the descendants of David and Solomon.

Israel descended into idol worship immediately, giving rise to prophets warning them of the consequences of their actions and almost universally warning of the destruction and deportation of the nation.

Judah gravitated back and forth between the legitimate worship of Yahweh and similar idol worship, provoking prophets to deliver a similar message to them as had been given in the north. Micah, one of these prophets, arose toward the end of the days of Judah and was a contemporary of the famous prophet Isaiah. While the message of the book of Micah centers on judgment of the shortcomings of the nation, the prophet also urges a return to the right kind of life that honors God.

In this specific passage, Micah draws attention to the fact that while many in Judah brought the right kind of sacrifices according to the Jewish law, their attitudes, thoughts, and manner of living did not line up with what they said. Acting badly toward their fellow Jews, cheating merchants out of what they were rightly due, and looking down on others did not honor God, and in essence invalidated whatever they thought they were accomplishing in their worship.[7]

The Point:

As was the case with the religious leaders of Christ's own day, many times there is a substantial disconnect between an individual's devotion toward God and their dealings with the people around them. Jesus Himself quoted Hosea 6:6 to them, "I desire mercy, not sacrifice," which reflects the same thought process expressed in the verse in Micah.

In other words, the vitality, depth, and quality of a person's relationship with God Himself is inseparably tied to the manner in which they act toward other people. Some prominent Christian leaders over the years have spoken in loud, shrill condemnations toward one another, specific entertainment personalities, people groups, political figures, and classes of society.

Ironically, some of these same leaders themselves have experienced humiliation when their own personal faults were brought to light. Jesus, by contrast, did not make loud public proclamations about the faults and flaws of others, but demonstrated true compassion both in words and concrete actions. When it comes to perfection, all of us are "equal opportunity offenders"!

Every day we make mistakes, have lapses in decision-making, draw the wrong conclusions, say the wrong words, or act disappointingly toward someone else. Described in the simplest of terms (though often the most difficult to accomplish) is the manner in which Christ Himself wants us to live out our lives.

First, to act justly, that is, fairly, in any and all matters that we have to deal with; that extends to church life, to work, to how we interact with our next-door neighbors, how we treat our family members, the way in which we do our jobs, and so on. Nothing in our daily lives is exempt from living in an honorable manner.

Second, we must love mercy, which by definition is not giving someone what they deserve (or what we *think* they deserve). This means that when the cashier asks for proper identification at the checkout line, instead of fussing or, worse, pitching a fit, we practice courtesy. It means when driving in rush our traffic that we avoid using sign language or greeting other idiots—I mean, drivers—by assigning any number of fanciful nicknames to them.

It also means that when a waitress messes up our order or the cook burns the pizza that we do not take it out on them. I am not advocating smiling and pretending that we act like everything is wonderful and not call out a mistake, but we can still do that in a way that shows consideration and respect for other people.

One of the greatest casualties in modern American life is courtesy and respect; instead of showing that consistently, most of us seem to find new ways in which to get offended.

Finally, we need to walk humbly with God; compared to Christ we all are equally imperfect and cannot truly live effectively without Him. We need to acknowledge our need for Him constantly and ask for His help every moment of every day, not just at worship, but all throughout our days.

Questions

1. Recall one of your personal experiences of rejection (e.g. a breakup, divorce, forced termination at work, etc.). Write out a one- or two-word description of how that felt and the ways in which it impacted your life.

2. Write down the names of 3–5 people with whom you deeply disagree, and consider the answers to the following questions for each:

   - What specific issues do you disagree over and why?

   - What opinions or beliefs do you have in common?

   - Do you like them personally? Why or why not?

   - How can you change your interactions with this person the very next time that you see them?

Write down the things that come to mind in situations where you have felt condemned, criticized, rejected, or judged. Pick one of the words and describe the ways in which you would rather have been treated. How can you change your own behavior to be positive more often toward others in your life?

What personal characteristics, habits, or hang-ups do you dislike in yourself? Why do they bother you? Which ones could you change or have you tried to change?

How can you apply the principles of acceptance to include yourself? What are ways you can affirm your own individual personhood?

Prayer

Lord, You demonstrated the most loving ways in dealing with those around You as You walked the earth; You made each one feel completely and totally valued, accepted, and important. You did not give blind approval to everyone's lifestyles or choices but still engaged them in a way that demonstrated profound respect. Use my life on an everyday basis to demonstrate that same respect to those I encounter.

Help me to look past behaviors and actions to the personhood of everyone I come in contact with, even when I am looking in the mirror. Let others see the face of Jesus Christ in mine, no matter who they are, where they come from, or even how they may choose to act toward me. When they interact with me, let them experience the unexpected and be the better for it. Make me more like You with every day, every hour, and every moment, from this day forward. Teach me to act justly, to love mercy, and to walk humbly with You. In Jesus's name, Amen.

Tug of War: Moving Past Judgment

It's not whether you get knocked down; it's whether you get back up.

Vince Lombardi

Church camp was the most celebrated time of the summer—a chance to get away from our parents and truly experience the joy of participating in all kinds of unique activities. I usually chose the ones that were crafty in nature and less physical: weaving placemats, painting T-shirts, designing pot holders, sewing socks that resembled baby chicks, or spinning little yarn pompoms.

In the awkwardness of those preteen years, this is where I felt safe and comfortable—no bathing suits, no horses, no rock climbing, and absolutely nothing that involved getting really dirty on purpose.

No matter how I felt, though, there were certain activities that everyone was required to participate in. I was certain that the camp counselors made them up and never told anyone until thirty minutes before the activity (torture) was to begin.

When I was eleven, the mandatory activity was a tug of war over a big pit of mud. The counselors were very excited and so were most of the boys that were attending camp. The girls on the other hand were split and begrudgingly participated.

The sides were picked, and the lines were drawn. The line-up was smallest in front, largest in back, which meant that the smallest members in front were drug back and forth through the mud pit repeatedly until one side eventually pulled the other side in entirely. I, of course, was very, very small…

— *Brenda*

Understanding the mind of judgmental people is one thing, but it does not supply much comfort from the injuries following an "attack" by one of them. For some, the wounds are somewhat superficial and amount to little more than a skinned knee or a paper cut; for others, the hurts leave deep gashes giving permanent scars that can last a lifetime. Psychologists, therapists, and counselors often quote the five stages of grief at this point, namely, denial, anger, bargaining, depression, and acceptance.[1] While knowing this may help map out the experience, something more practical will likely bring more tangible comfort.

I held my breath as the votes were counted at the church meeting where everything came to a head, and when it was clear that the vote just barely ousted me, I was stunned—probably more like deeply numb. After leaving the building that evening, I stole a real estate "for sale" sign and jammed it into the rocky soil of my front yard, the building where the church had once met. Getting past the deep pain from the experience took longer than it should have, mostly because I managed to get in my own way.

The experience burned me out to such a degree that it brought on personal health issues that resulted in my leaving public ministry. I credit three significant influences in guiding me down the road to a healthy recovery—the LORD Jesus Christ (my Savior and example); my wife, Brenda (my best and forever friend); and Brooklake Community Church, where I have attended for the past eleven years.

Moving past these kinds of personal experiences requires more than just merely surviving; to me the term implies barely escaping something and being diminished by it. Fortunately, the Bible itself furnishes relevant examples of others who braved such hardships and emerged stronger as a result.

Perhaps the greatest case in point is the life of Joseph, recorded in the closing chapters of the book of Genesis, specifically chapters 38 through 50. Jacob, like his father, Isaac, played favorites and elevated Joseph to a position of both favor and prominence, due to the fact that he was the firstborn son of his favorite wife, Rachel.

It didn't help matters that at seventeen years old, Joseph apparently possessed no tact whatsoever, nor a sound sense of how to deal with relationships. Ten of his brothers openly hated him and, in fact, at one point plotted to actually kill him and blame some wild animal (almost sounds like an episode of *The Jerry Springer*

Show). The fate of this young man is summarized in the following verses from Genesis chapter 37:23–36.

> So when Joseph came to his brothers, they stripped him of his robe—the richly ornamented robe he was wearing- and they took him and threw him into the cistern. Now the cistern was empty; there was no water in it. As they sat down to eat their meal, they looked up and saw a caravan of Ishmael-ites coming from Gilead. Their camels were loaded with spices, balm and myrrh, and they were on their way to take them down to Egypt. Judah said to his brothers, "What will we gain if we kill our brother and cover up his blood? Come, let's sell him to the Ishmaelites and not lay our hands on him; after all, he is our brother, our own flesh and blood."
>
> His brothers agreed. So when the Midianite mer-chants came by, his brothers pulled Joseph up out of the cistern and sold him for twenty shekels of silver to the Ishmaelites, who took him to Egypt. When Reuben returned to the cistern and saw that Joseph was not there, he tore his clothes. He went back to his brothers and said, "The boy isn't there! Where can I turn now?" Then they got Joseph's robe, slaughtered a goat and dipped the robe in the blood. They took the ornamented robe back to their father and said, "We found this. Examine it to see whether it is your son's robe." He recognized it and said, "It is my son's robe! Some ferocious ani-mal has devoured him. Joseph has surely been torn to pieces."

Then Jacob tore his clothes, put on sackcloth and mourned for his son many days. All his sons and daughters came to comfort him, but he refused to be comforted. "No," he said, "in mourning will I go down to the grave to my son." So his father wept for him. Meanwhile, the Midianites sold Joseph in Egypt to Potiphar, one of Pharaoh's officials, the captain of the guard.

Judah saw selling the hated brother into a life of slavery as the ultimate solution to all of their problems; they permanently got rid of a rival and someone they couldn't stand, and they did not have to feel the guilt involved in his death. By examining the outcome of this deeply hurtful act and my own personal healing process, we can get a sense of how to move past these negative experiences. The process involves about six principles that can help facilitate this.

1. Acknowledge the Hurt

2. Give Yourself Time

3. Don't Pick at Your Scabs

4. Let the Train Leave the Station

5. Understand the Nature of Cause and Effect

6. Use Your Hurt to Heal Others

Acknowledge the Hurt

While it may seem obvious, you need to squarely face the fact that you have been hurt; pretending that it never happened, that you had it coming, or just trying to outrun it, just delays the healing process. As you try to address the whole situation facing you, expect to bounce up and down the entire range of the emotional spectrum. At times, you will feel deeply hurt and feel grief; at others, you will feel anger and perhaps even rage, and you will naturally want to dish out heaping portions of blame toward yourself, those that hurt you, and, yes, even God Himself.

Joseph certainly felt a whole range of emotions as he experienced the unthinkable. He heard his big brother Judah negotiating his sale price as he was reduced to mere currency. Joseph then was dragged against his will to a place he knew nothing about. Finally he listened as some foreigner called out bids for him as he stood at an auction for his very life. Even the most mature seventeen-year-old would feel a sense of deep betrayal, hurt, fear, and anger. In my own experience, I expected God to look down from heaven, pronounce judgment, and leave a proverbial crater in the place where the church stood, particularly after I found out that they changed the locks.

Like Jonah, I fumed at God for seemingly doing nothing and letting people off scot-free, never paying the price for inflicting deliberate hurt. In time, I gained an entirely new understanding and perspective, but at least at the time I acknowledged what happened and how it felt, as Joseph no doubt did.

Give Yourself Time

Speaking in general terms, healing is a process that takes a while to move through. One case in point happens when you and I get a scrape or cut (a mild injury) or when broken bones begin to mend (a somewhat longer process). From a physical standpoint I experienced this when knocked off a mountain bike. My left ring finger had a fracture as well as deep gashes, and my right shoulder had separated, requiring surgery; the cuts healed first, then the finger, followed by the shoulder.

None of this occurred overnight; broken feelings have to heal in the same precise manner. Anyone that has lost a close loved one or experienced a difficult break up can attest to that fact. Healing from my own brush with judgmental people has taken well over a decade and happened in various stages. As much as any of us would like to rush the process and get to "the good stuff," time has to pass for the hurt to sting less. In reality, there will always be "bad days," but the good news is that the interval *between* these times gradually gets greater and greater.

Again, the life of Joseph draws this point out as well; at seventeen his brothers sold him as a slave, and he did not lay eyes on them again for another twenty years or so, probably close to age forty. In the intervening period of time, Joseph managed to come to grips with the wrong done to him, evidenced by his own words in Genesis 41:50–52:

Before the years of famine came, two sons were born to Joseph by Asenath daughter of Potiphera, priest of On. Joseph named his firstborn Manasseh and said, "It is because God has made me forget all my trouble and all my father's household." The second son he named Ephraim and said, "It is because God has made me fruitful in the land of my suffering."

You don't get a sense of anger or bitterness in Joseph's words, but rather a sense of coming to terms and even implying a sense of forgiveness; in fact, this gives the impression of someone that has finally turned the corner regarding a haunting chapter of his life. This is consistent with human experience and gives us a glimpse of the best way to process hurt and recover.

Don't Pick at Your Scabs

Sure, the phrase sounds gross, but it vividly illustrates the point—reliving the experience over and over, dissecting it in your mind and holding on to it simply keeps the wounds fresh and prevents the healing process from setting in. Probably the biggest side effect of living in the past is bitterness, in which we essentially hold a grudge; the result brings harm not to those who hurt us, but to ourselves instead. Stop trying to deconstruct the experience—what could I have done better, how could I have avoided it—this thinking is a waste of time.

I tried to imagine the outcome if the situation had gone the opposite direction, if I had just quit before the problems began, but in reality it does not add anything to either the healing process or any sense of wellbeing. One of the dialogues from *The Matrix Reloaded*, makes this point rather succinctly as follows:

> MORPHEUS: "What happened, happened as it should have happened, and couldn't have happened any other way."

> NEO: "How do you know?"

> MORPHEUS: "We are still alive."[2]

In my younger days, I tried to focus on just doing everything perfectly, and as is the case with most perfectionists, I was under the illusion that executing every action with calculated perfection would remove me from blame or criticism. After spending some time processing the church experience, however, I discovered something rather profound.

To begin with, none of us possess the capability to do everything flawlessly, let alone with ongoing consistency. In addition, only One, Jesus Christ, fully God and fully human, lived a sinless and perfect life. Although He possessed no moral, personal, or spiritual defects and lived a perfect life, other people felt personally threatened, still found fault, and had Jesus executed as a common criminal. If Christ didn't stand a chance of actually *being* perfect, what on earth makes us think that we do?

Let the Train Leave
the Station

In other words, move on, and leave it all behind, which begins with a simple (and often difficult) act of forgiveness; the simple truth of the matter is that forgiveness does not excuse the offender, but rather it frees the one that has been hurt. One of the most poignant scenes portraying this comes from Tyler Perry's 2005 movie, *Diary of a Mad Black Woman*. The dialogue takes place between Helen, whose attorney husband literally threw her out on the street after eighteen years, and her mother, Myrtle, as follows:

> MYRTLE: "You know I know this man put a hurtin' on you baby, but you've got to forgive him. No matter what he's done, you've got to forgive him— not for him, but for you."
>
> HELEN: "Forgive him for me?"
>
> MYRTLE: "When somebody hurts you they take power over you, if you don't forgive them then they keeps the power. Forgive him, baby, and after you forgive him, forgive yourself."[3]

Forgiveness does indeed free us and allows real healing to begin; think of how the body operates when we have a splinter in a finger or toe. We can treat the wound endlessly, but until we remove the offending sliver of wood, the wound stays fresh; truly forgiving the other person is like removing the splinter from our hearts, so to speak. As a part of that process, ask God specifically to heal you of the hurt.

During the earthly ministry of Jesus, He made it a regular practice to perform miraculous healings—blindness, illness, inability to walk, and even death. What Christ did for the physical body in those events, He is fully capable of doing to the human heart, even though the wound may run particularly deep.

Keeping a journal can help in the process, along with joining a group where you can share feelings in a safe setting. Christ created us for relationships, and by joining together with other compassionate people of faith that recovery can come more readily and quickly.

Once again, Joseph clearly forgave the seemingly unforgivable acts committed against him. As the second in command of the entire nation of Egypt, he possessed the ability to have every one of them executed with no repercussions whatsoever. Instead, once Joseph confirmed that his brothers had truly changed, he demonstrated true forgiveness to them, in Genesis 45:3–8:

> Joseph said to his brothers, "I am Joseph! Is my father still living?" But his brothers were not able to answer him, because they were terrified at his presence. Then Joseph said to his brothers, "Come close to me." When they had done so, he said, "I am your brother Joseph, the one you sold into Egypt!
>
> And now, do not be distressed and do not be angry with yourselves for selling me here, because it was to save lives that God sent me ahead of you. For

two years now there has been famine in the land, and for the next five years there will not be plowing and reaping. But God sent me ahead of you to preserve for you a remnant on earth and to save your lives by a great deliverance. "So then, it was not you who sent me here, but God. He made me father to Pharaoh, Lord of his entire household and ruler of all Egypt."

Joseph had the opportunity for immediate revenge with no consequences, yet he chose to treat them with kindness, forgiveness, and even love. Granted, his brothers were terrified (Who wouldn't be?), but the scene portrayed in this passage is a glad reunion, made possible by an imperfect person demonstrating forgiveness of other imperfect people.

Another important lesson from these verses shows that Joseph had taken a larger view of the events as creating something far greater in God's ultimate plans, "So it was not you who sent me here, but God." Understand at this point that God is without fault, flaw, or shortcoming, and is not responsible for the evil that happens to us or all around us. In the midst of that, however, you and I can learn valuable life lessons as well as become part of the greater purpose of God in the world around us. [4]

Understand the Nature of Cause and Effect

Often, though not always, individuals or groups demonstrate recurring patterns of hurtful behavior toward others. With that being the case, the chances are rather good that their judgmental and mean-spirited thoughts, words, and actions actually have nothing to do with you at all; you just happen to be in the wrong place at the wrong time, so to speak.

My pastor, Mike Axton, describes this with the phrase "Hurt people... hurt people"; in other words, human beings who have experienced great hurt and personal pain can easily inflict that same sense of injury toward others. Frequently, however, that results in a life filled with broken relationships, loneliness, alienation, and many other negative outcomes; in other words, those who habitually inflict pain on the lives of others end up carrying the consequences of their behaviors in a very real sense.

In science, this is referred to as the law of cause and effect, expressed in the writings of Paul in the New Testament with the words, "A man reaps what he sows" (Galatians 6:7b). Actions create inevitable consequences in every area of life, and no one is exempt from that simple fact of universal human experience.

Joseph's brothers sold him as a slave and got away with it, but they clearly held on to huge amounts of regret in the process, even almost two decades after the fact. When they showed up to buy grain in Egypt, Joseph began putting them to the test to see if they had really changed, resulting in the following response from them:

> They said to one another, "Surely we are being punished because of our brother. We saw how distressed he was when he pleaded with us for his life, but we would not listen; that's why this distress has come upon us." Reuben replied, "Didn't I tell you not to sin against the boy? But you wouldn't listen! Now we must give an accounting for his blood." They did not realize that Joseph could understand them, since he was using an interpreter.
>
> Genesis 42:21–22 (NIV)

Every one of these men carried tremendous guilt, and clearly the memories still carried vivid, painful details for them. Even after Joseph revealed himself to them and granted them forgiveness, they still carried significant fear, expecting him to exact some type of revenge. After their father, Jacob, died a number of years later, they still expected retribution (Review Genesis 50:15–21 for the details).

I learned this firsthand a couple of years ago when I actually went back and visited the church in Tennessee referenced at the very beginning of this book. As my family and I walked into the building, I felt butterflies, as the last time there had been unpleasantly memorable. I recognized a great number of the people, who were all glad to see me; we did not inform anyone that we were coming, so the fact that most of the families involved in the effort previously described were not there that day was rather amazing.

The current pastor made a point of recognizing me during the service, thanked me for my efforts, and even asked me to close the service in prayer. Even more amazing, a young man with a pregnant wife told me that years earlier when I regularly visited his parents, that he had been listening on the upstairs balcony and that led to his commitment to Christ. The experience truly healed me, and the pastor at that time confided that the church even until that day had experienced difficulty trusting the pastoral leadership in general, which had hindered its ability to grow. Ironically, that revelation did not bring any feeling of vindication, but rather of a sense of sadness, but it certainly shows how consequences always follow actions.

Use Your Hurt to Heal Others

In the lives of followers of Jesus Christ, no experience is ever wasted, neither the great victories, grand accomplishments, hardships, nor colossal mistakes go unaddressed or unused in our lives. When you experience harsh and judgmental attitudes and actions at the hands of others, it gives you a profound appreciation of how others feel when you interact with them. Some hurts are obviously unintentional, teaching us how to act sensitively toward those around us. Others may be inflicted intentionally, allowing us to sympathize with others who have lived through similar situations.

My own painful experiences have created an immediate bond with many people outside church life, and provided me numerous opportunities to assist other people who have lived through the same thing. When you have the chance to better someone else's life by sharing what you have gone through, it not only makes a huge difference for them, but it allows your own healing to become that much more certain. My own personal hope is that by sharing my own story throughout the covers of this book will bring hope, healing, and recovery to others.

Joseph had the benefit of time to put the pieces of the puzzle together in his own mind long before he ever saw his brothers again; very likely, he never expected to lay eyes on them during his lifetime. Joseph's own words to his brothers—"You intended to harm me, but God intended it for good"—speak volumes not only about his own perspective, but also about understanding how those experiences brought incredible benefit to many people.

Egypt at the time had an abundance of food, which was not the case for other countries in the region. Joseph learned how to run the economic and business affairs of a nation because he had learned to run a business (Potiphar's household) and a government institution (the Egyptian federal prison, their version of Leavenworth).

He also experienced some rather brutal and unjust abuse to get to that point, namely being sold into slavery by his brothers, imprisoned on false rape charges, and being forgotten by people of influence. In retrospect, Joseph could easily have become jaded and untrusting and, speaking from the human side of the equation, no one would have blamed him. Instead, he used the life lessons that he learned from the "school of hard knocks" and as a result, used his considerable power and influence to help his family, the nation, and region at large.

Going Deeper

A psalm of David. When he fled from his son Absalom.

O LORD, how many are my foes! How many rise up against me! Many are saying of me, "God will not deliver him." Selah. But you are a shield around me, O LORD; you bestow glory on me and lift up my head. To the LORD I cry aloud, and he answers me from his holy hill. Selah. I lie down and sleep; I wake again, because the LORD sustains me. I will not fear the tens of thousands drawn up against me on every side. Arise, O LORD! Deliver me, O my God! Strike all my enemies on the jaw; break the teeth of the wicked. From the LORD comes deliverance. May your blessing be on your people. Selah.

Psalm 3:1–8 (NIV)

Background:

Israelite history regards David as the greatest king ever to rule the nation, with no close seconds; Solomon certainly brought the country to its economic and political height, but due in large part to the preparation David had made. Even so, David was human and far from perfection, and his worst personal incident involved Bathsheba and the convenient killing of her husband.

While David admitted his wrongdoing in no uncertain terms, this sparked the beginning of an entire string of personal difficulties in his life, not the least of which was a *coup d'état* led by his oldest living son, Absalom. Solomon may have inherited the throne, but Absalom clearly inherited the lion's share of David's military abilities.

Second Samuel chapters 15–18 provide the details on how the deed was done and the fallout that resulted. One of the interesting side notes of the entire experience was the defection of several people in David's administration to the takeover campaign by Absalom. An advisor named Ahithophel, possibly a blood relative of Bathsheba, used intimate knowledge of David's capabilities to give the usurper a competitive edge in the conflict; since he had counted the man as a close personal friend, this breach had a particularly sharp edge to it.

David penned this particular psalm during his hasty escape from Jerusalem, when the emotions ran fresh. While his faith in Yahweh to deliver him comes through loud and clear, so does the obvious pain and anguish included in the request for rather substantial harm on his personal adversaries.[4]

The Point:

None of us have the luxury of escaping difficulties in life, regardless of how smart, successful, powerful, or even spiritual we may be. One of the hallmarks of human existence is the fact that life is both fragile and unpredictable, due in large part to the simple consequence of dealing with imperfect people.

As we grew up, we experienced parents, friends, and relatives who failed to meet our expectations, broke promises, or just didn't live up to what we thought they would do. When the hurt and disappointment runs deep, you and I need more than just a pat on the back from a well-meaning friend telling us it "will all be okay."

Jesus Himself walked on the earth in full humanity, and experienced all of the proverbial bumps and bruises of life, particularly at the hands of other people. Judas, whom He had counted as a friend, accepted a financial payoff to hand Him over to the Jewish authorities.

At the same time, the rest of His closest companions all ran off in the hour of Christ's greatest need; the sting of that abandonment had to heighten the difficulty of the situation all the more. When others inflict pain on us, intentionally or unintentionally, no one understands our feelings more than Jesus Himself; at those moments, just talking to Him and pouring out your anguish and disappointment is something He welcomes.

Just like David fleeing from the intentions of his own son, you can express those emotions, whether verbally or in the form of a journal, and that can go a long way to starting the process of getting past the experience.

> … The kingdom of heaven is like a king who wanted to settle accounts with his servants. As he began the settlement, a man who owed him ten thousand bags of gold was brought to him. Since he was not able to pay, the master ordered that he and his wife and his children and all that he had be sold to repay the debt. "The servant fell on his knees before him. 'Be patient with me,' he begged, 'and I will pay back everything.' The servant's master took pity on him, canceled the debt and let him go. "But when that servant went out, he found one of his fellow servants who owed him a hundred silver coins. He grabbed him and began to choke him. 'Pay back what you owe me!' he demanded. "His fellow servant fell to his knees and begged him, 'Be patient with me, and I will pay you back.' "But he refused… Then the master called the servant in. 'You wicked servant,' he said, 'I canceled all that debt of yours because you begged me to. Shouldn't you have had mercy on your fellow servant just as I had on you?' In anger his master handed him over to the jailers to be tortured, until he should pay back all he owed. "This is how my heavenly Father will treat each of you unless you forgive a brother or sister from your heart."

> Matthew 18:21–35 (NIV)

Background:

Peter came to Jesus with a practical question about forgiveness, asking at what point that reached a limit. The rabbis and teachers of that time considered the maximum number of times that someone should grant a repeating offender was three; Peter probably thought he was demonstrating extraordinary generosity by suggesting seven, well over twice that! Jesus responded by teaching that such forgiveness should extend even further, to seventy-seven—not intended as the actual limit, but to make the point that forgiving needs to be infinite. To vividly illustrate the point, Christ began telling another parable, this one involving debt.

During the period of first century Roman rule, the practice was common that individuals who failed to repay borrowed amounts of money would end up having all their possessions liquidated and were thrown into prison. Needless to say, if this took place today, most creditors would end up wealthy and more than half of the U.S. population would be in jail! In any case, the first servant owed a staggering amount of money, equivalent to over $30,000,000 today, and even with seemingly hundreds of years of labor, it would be impossible to repay.

As the man faced the worst possible consequences, he threw himself on the mercy of the master to whom the debt was due; the master felt pity for him and canceled the entire amount owing, not only suggesting great compassion but also considerable wealth. Feeling great relief, the newly liberated servant left the building and ran into a friend, who also worked for the same master, and demanded payment for what probably amounted to $60.00. When his fellow employee asked for mercy (just as he had to his master), he refused and threw the man in jail.

Well, bad news travels fast, and when the benefactor found out what happened, he was understandably livid, making the point that since he had received great forgiveness, he should have granted it as well. The story ends much as it began, but this time with the indebted servant carrying out a harsh sentence. Jesus ends with the simple point that as human beings we should not hold grudges and fail to grant mercy to others, since God has granted forgiveness freely to us.[5]

The Point:

As imperfect beings, you and I commit acts of stupidity, insensitivity, and downright meanness more times a day than we could possibly ever count or realize. The Bible uses the term *sin* and also makes the point that this creates separation from the person and presence of God.

Even on a good day we would still commit screw ups, and Jesus Christ came to pay the price and penalty due to each one of us so that our debt would be clear, forgiven, and gone, erased just as if clearing a blackboard. In reality, the amount and number of the sins we commit in a lifetime would conservatively take advanced scientific notation to record, just as massive a debt as pictured by the first servant in the parable.

When we experience the forgiveness from God through the sacrifice of Jesus Christ on the cross, nothing remains, and we are free. As other people do not so nice things to us, we need to extend forgiveness to them, just as Christ granted great forgiveness to us. When we compare the "scores" of what we have been cleared of versus what we should clear others of personally, it's minute by comparison. If we fail to grant to others what we have experienced, it carries grave consequences, just as in the story.

> Some time later, Jesus went up to Jerusalem for one of the Jewish festivals. Now there is in Jerusalem near the Sheep Gate a pool, which in Aramaic is called Bethesda and which is surrounded by five covered colonnades. Here a great number of disabled people used to lie—the blind, the lame, the paralyzed. One who was there had been an invalid for thirty-eight years. When Jesus saw him lying there and learned that he had been in this condition for a long time, he asked him, "Do you want to get well?" "Sir," the invalid replied, "I have no one to help me into the pool when the water is stirred. While I am trying to get in, someone else goes down ahead of me." Then Jesus said to him, "Get up! Pick up your mat and walk." At once the man was cured; he picked up his mat and walked.
>
> John 5:1–8 (NIV)

Background:

As a faithful Jew, Jesus attended all of feasts required of adult men in Palestine; attendance was mandatory and took place at the temple in the city of Jerusalem. One of the areas within the building attracted those with incurable illnesses and physical issues, because of a local legend that when an angel made the water move, the first person to get in would be cured.

One of the disabled individuals there had been ill for nearly forty years, and, as Jesus approached him, He asked if he wanted to get well. The sight of a large group of severely ill people must have been overpowering, and I seriously doubt that anyone asked that question would have said no. Whether the man was born with that condition or developed it later is not clear, but the fact that he desperately wanted to get well is.

Jesus healed him on the spot, and he stood to his feet. What may escape your notice is that this miraculous healing has two aspects. The first aspect involved the correction of whatever physical conditions that took away his ability to walk to begin with, whether neurological, circulatory, deformity-related, and such.

The second, and less obvious, miracle involved in the knowledge and ability to walk; whether he had ever walked or simply had been off his feet for thirty eight years, he would have had to learn to walk again. Therapists assist patients in doing this today, and it can take a while for it to happen successfully, just as when a baby begins walking. In this case, the man instantly had that capability, given as part of the healing that Jesus provided by God's power. [6]

JOSEPH RINEHART & BRENDA RINEHART

The Point:

The desire and ability of Jesus to heal has not changed; at times these physical healings take place through the hands of physicians, nurses, and therapists, and at other times rather miraculous healings happen that can boost the faith of many. The human heart has the same ability to break as the skin and bones most often bumped and bruised. Jesus desired to heal not just the body but the soul or inner person as well. As He asked the disabled man, "Do you want to get well?"

Christ also asks you and I today—do we want to have our broken hearts mended, our bruised feelings healed, and our emotional wounds soothed? Of all the injuries that a human being can endure, a broken heart is probably without equal the worst that we experience—certainly the multitude of country music songs can attest to that! Since God cares intimately about every aspect of our existence, it makes perfect sense that He cares about hurts in our hearts and souls as well.

Jesus came to bring every one of us a *full and abundant* life, not just an existence that we try our best to merely endure. Even in our worst experiences of judgment by others, or the purposeful infliction of harm by others for all sorts of reasons, Jesus Christ wants to bring healing, recovery, and joy to us!

Questions

1. What are the three greatest hurtful experiences you can recall in your life? Rank them in order, and answer the following questions about the experience:

- How long ago did this take place?

- Who was involved? What did they do that hurt you?

- How does that experience negatively impact your life today?

- Do you find yourself still holding on to the pain?

- How can you let that go?

- What unique ability can this give you to help others in similar situations?

2. When have you been the offender and brought hurt and pain to someone else? Have you forgiven yourself? Have you asked the other person for forgiveness?

3. How do you try to cope with personal hurt? Is that effective? What "side effects" does your coping mechanism have, if any?

4. When was the last time you healed from an injury? What did the experience feel like? How can you apply that to getting over hurt feelings? Have you ever asked Christ to bring healing to your broken heart?

JOSEPH RINEHART & BRENDA RINEHART

5. What can you do to behave in a more Christ like manner toward others, even (and especially) when they may not deserve it? How can your life reflect the compassion, forgiveness, and mercy of God? Why is that important to you, other people, and the larger world around you?

Prayer

LORD, I know that living in this world can often bring disappointment, hurt, and personal pain. Give me the strength to forgive others when they hurt me, regardless of whether it is intentional or unintentional, whether they ask for forgiveness or not, and whether they are friend or foe. Heal my many hurts, the ones from long ago, the ones that I feel today, and the ones yet to come.

Give me a heart of compassion and understanding that grants forgiveness to all, including myself. Reveal Your love to me, through me, and beyond me. Perform a new work in my life this very moment, helping me to realize that You completely accept me and love me, and reach others through me for the sake of Your love, Your kingdom, and all the future has to hold. In Jesus's name, Amen.

Capture the Flag: Putting It All Together

> Never criticize a man until you've walked a mile in his moccasins.
>
> Native American Proverb

The game of Capture the Flag could be summed up in the phrase, "To the winner go the spoils." As a child of the late sixties and seventies, Capture the Flag was played with an old sock tied to a limb we broke off the tree in the backyard, and a handful of Nerf balls because the girls were playing, and no one was allowed to get hurt. I am not even sure we fully understood the complexity of the game, as we hid crouched behind the trees waiting for the next victim from the opposing team to wander into our trap. We didn't strategize or even plan anything past, "You stand here, and I'll climb that tree over there."

Fast-forward thirty-five years and the game is far more advanced. "Capture the Flag, well, sure I know how to play." Those words tumbled from my lips before I discovered that my teenage daughter's version of this game was complete with paint ball guns and a field equipped with fox holes and barricades. These things are necessary because paint balls hurt at a decent range, and at close range they hurt a lot. I failed to mention the Nerf balls to her, and as it turned out my daughter won the game, and since I was on her team, cowering in terror behind the barricade, I won too.

— *Brenda*

Remember the phone call from the "concerned" church leader in Tennessee at the opening of the book? Looking back, that marked the beginning of the end, so to speak; the point at which someone a little more experienced would have read the proverbial handwriting on the wall, seen the gathering storm clouds, resigned, and left. Instead, being young and still idealistic, I tried to engage the issues and assumed that some kind of compromise could be forged.

Numerous closed-door meetings followed with heated discussions on about every topic imaginable, and rumors started circulating that a church planter was only supposed to stay two years anyway. Strictly speaking, the Southern Baptist Home Mission Board (as it was called at that time) provided funding for a two-year period, but nothing definitive existed mandating some version of "term limits."

This rumor reflected some attempt to legitimize my exit as the church planter/pastor and solidify their particular cultural agenda with no more resistance. In the eventual course of events, the sponsoring church pushed holding a vote for whether or not I would remain as pastor once the mission church was on its own. At the end, I lost out by five votes, which delighted the people who had wanted a "good old fashioned" traditional Baptist church but terribly upset the rest of the people who had enjoyed the direction of something more progressive and inclusive.

A number of the members and attendees that spoke to me in the days following expressed shock, as they had been given the impression that it was merely a formality and that my job was never in question. To make matters worse, I tried to take the high road by delivering a sermon on the power of forgiveness, but for some reason the now-victorious crowd was offended, and I was terminated immediately after. The locks on the church were changed soon after that, and I didn't set foot in that building again, until that visit made years later when God arranged it so that the group that ousted me happened to be out of town that Sunday.

Other than the divorce of my parents, this series of events marked the most painful and difficult in my life up to that point. I had taken a stand on what I believed—and still believe—was on the right side, honoring God and trying to positively impact the lives of people around me. Any pastor, leader, or church member that has survived a similar circumstance understands the personal, spiritual, and relational toll that it takes. When looking at the clash between Jesus and the religious leaders of His own day, one gains a whole new appreciation of what He went through and the principles that he taught. In short, Jesus taught by example and by word how humans should live and treat one another. In Matthew 22:34–40, He laid out the foundational teachings using the following words:

> Hearing that Jesus had silenced the Sadducees, the Pharisees got together. One of them, an expert in the law, tested him with this question: "Teacher, which is the greatest commandment in the Law?" Jesus replied: " Love the LORD your God with all your heart and with all your soul and with all your mind.' This is the first and greatest commandment. And the second is like it: 'Love your neighbor as yourself.' All the Law and the Prophets hang on these two commandments."

Jesus summed up the entire responsibility of human beings toward God with two priorities. First, the focus must be on God Himself, not on us or anything/anyone else. The real problem with people is their imperfections. Part of the reason people can get into judging games is that they begin comparing themselves to one another—inevitably you can always find those much worse, as well as those that are better, and this applies to any and every area of life (a form of pride).

When we look to God (who is perfect) as the standard, we understand that we can never measure up on our own, and it's a lot simpler to see other people in the same light. Without God we cannot do anything on our own, and we can easily say, "But for the grace of God, there go I."

The second priority is how we relate to others, and the Pharisees in other passages wanted to split hairs on the definition of "neighbor"—prompting the parable of the Good Samaritan, which took it beyond the "accepted" people to any person that we have the ability to help. It's not a coincidence that Jesus picked a class/race of people that the Jews despised. God's love is demonstrated through us as we deal with other people, not merely sitting behind a hymnal telling Him how great He is.

It's easy to throw rocks at ultra-religious people and find fault, but the fact is that even those that have experienced mistreatment by "church lady" types can act in the same manner without realizing it. Again, looking at how Jesus treated people serves as a vivid example, this time looking at one of the "Rambo" of outcasts, a tax-collector named Zacchaeus, in Luke 19:1–9:

> Jesus entered Jericho and was passing through. A man was there by the name of Zacchaeus; he was a chief tax collector and was wealthy. He wanted to see who Jesus was, but because he was short he could not see over the crowd. So he ran ahead and climbed a sycamore-fig tree to see him, since Jesus was coming that way. When Jesus reached the spot, he looked up and said to him, "Zacchaeus, come down immediately. I must stay at your house today." So he came down at once and welcomed him gladly. All the people saw this and began to mutter, "He has gone to be the guest of a sinner." But Zacchaeus stood up and said to the LORD, "Look, LORD! Here and now I give half of

my possessions to the poor, and if I have cheated anybody out of anything, I will pay back four times the amount." Jesus said to him, "Today salvation has come to this house, because this man, too, is a son of Abraham. For the Son of Man came to seek and to save what was lost."

Jesus's encounter with Zacchaeus is pretty consistent with other accounts recorded in the gospels. One of the most striking things that you can pick up is that He acted in the same manner with all people, regardless of status, social standing, reputation, or religious affiliation. In this regard, we need to emulate the character of Christ by treating everyone we encounter in the same way. As emphasized before, Jesus accepted each person as a creation of immense personal value and demonstrated that regard tangibly.

In the specific example quoted here, Jesus welcomed the opportunity to establish a relationship with this man, who was an outcast in every sense of the word; first, he had moral issues—tax collectors were not paid for their services, so they overcharged their customers and kept the difference. The fact that they worked for Rome made them hated already, and cheating people on top of that made it all the more heinous.

As a result they were not welcome at the synagogue, in social gatherings, in the community, or with any group. Even "common" folk such as the type of people represented by most of Jesus's followers did not willingly have any dealings with them. Jesus went to the house of Zacchaeus and spent time visiting and conversing with him, never once condoning his lifestyle or practices. In a surprising turn of events the man turned his entire life around and followed the teachings of Jesus.[1]

In this passage, it wasn't the religious establishment—the Pharisees and priests—that griped about Jesus going to the IRS agent's house. It was His own followers, the ones already despised by the Jewish leadership. Clearly, as individual human beings, we can easily make the same mistakes that we find offensive in others, just emphasizing that we are all equally fallible. Too many times, our culture in the United States glorifies confidence, certainty, independence, and strength to the point that a person might consider himself incapable of error.

Any truth taken to an extreme can result in issues; confidence and strength can be beneficial, but left unchecked can create arrogance. Each of us is an "equal opportunity offender" and capable of the same faults, imperfections, bad decisions, and capable of the same acts as anyone else. Viewing ourselves in this light helps us accept others instead of somehow being superior or better than those around us. It's a day-to-day journey that we all have to monitor. We never actually "arrive," but we can stay diligent to prevent falling into thinking and, subsequently, attitudes and actions.

To some, this may sound alarming and appear to rubber stamp everything as acceptable, diluting the precepts of biblical truth and opening the door to all sorts of erroneous teachings. Nothing could be further from reality; truth remains truth. The principles contained throughout this entire volume come solidly from the assumption that God chose to reveal Himself through the living Word, Jesus Christ, and the written Word, the Bible.

The concepts of personhood, values, acceptance, and the very example in the life of Jesus, presuppose the validity of these concepts. The focus of what we have talked about has had much more to do with relationships, how you and I view ourselves, how we view others, and ultimately the ways in which we choose to interact. Going back to my experience in Tennessee, if you had interviewed or surveyed everyone involved, I am almost certain that the doctrinal beliefs would have sounded remarkably similar.

Truths regarding God, the Bible, the significance of gathering together, and the importance of a living relationship with Jesus Christ would have topped every agenda. The thorny part of the equation was not the "what"—theological truth—but the "how" of the business of "doing church." One saying that is both relevant and popular is that the only army that shoots its own wounded are those claiming the name of Christ.

Where do you fall in the spectrum? Do you implicitly or explicitly find yourself carrying the attitude that your personal character, life, and relationship with God are somehow better than someone else's? Have you distanced yourself from "those other people" whose lives, beliefs, and life choices differ from your own?

Has your life revealed the compassion of Jesus Christ, or a more judgmental mindset and the actions that flow out of that? Remember, according to Jesus Himself, you and I cannot truly claim to love God without also loving those He created in His image. Can you

JOSEPH RINEHART & BRENDA RINEHART

retrain yourself to look for that image in the lives of others, in their eyes, and in the hearts that ironically have been broken by misguided churches and Christians? Only by doing that can it truly be said of us, that we "have our Father's eyes."

Going Deeper

Now Naaman was commander of the army of the king of Aram. He was a great man in the sight of his master and highly regarded, because through him the LORD had given victory to Aram. He was a valiant soldier, but he had leprosy. Now bands from Aram had gone out and had taken captive a young girl from Israel, and she served Naaman's wife. She said to her mistress, "If only my master would see the prophet who is in Samaria! He would cure him of his leprosy." Naaman went to his master and told him what the girl from Israel had said. "By all means, go," the king of Aram replied ... The letter that he took to the king of Israel read: "With this letter I am sending my servant Naaman to you so that you may cure him of his leprosy." As soon as the king of Israel read the letter, he tore his robes ... When Elisha the man of God heard that the king of Israel had torn his robes, he sent him this message: "Why have you torn your robes? Have the man come to me and he will know that there is a prophet in Israel." So Naaman went with his horses and chariots and stopped at the door of Elisha's house. Elisha sent a messenger to say to him, "Go, wash yourself seven times in the Jordan, and your flesh will be restored and you will be cleansed." But Naaman went away angry… Naaman's servants went to him and said, "My father, if the prophet had told you to do some great thing, would you not have done it? How much more, then, when he tells you, 'Wash and be cleansed'!" So he went down and dipped himself in the Jordan seven times, as the man of God had told him, and his flesh was restored and became clean like that of a young boy. Then Naaman and all his attendants went back to the man of God. He stood before him and said, "Now I know that there is no God in all the world except in Israel."

2 Kings 5:1–19 (NIV)

Background:

During the days of the divided kingdom (as explained before, the northern kingdom, Israel, and the southern kingdom, Judah), the military and political balance of power in the region shifted constantly. At times, Israel and Judah had bad relations and fought against one another, and at other times each had conflicts with bordering nations, such as Syria, referred to at times as Aram.

At this particular point in time, Israel (the northern kingdom) and Aram had a peace accord; although, apparently some minor skirmishes still occasionally happened on their shared border. During one of these scuffles, a young Israelite girl ended up captured and became a servant in the house of the commanding general of the army of Aram, a man named Naaman. Naaman had contracted leprosy, a disease hardly encountered these days, but in ancient times it amounted to a slow death sentence, in which the skin on the body slowly rotted in a revolting manner.

The young woman, freely sharing her faith in Yahweh, mentioned the prophet Elisha could easily heal the man's disease. Ben-Hadad, the king of Aram, got wind of this and sent Naaman to Jehoram, the king of Israel, with enough currency and clothing that would amount to about $1,247,240 (US) today.

Jehoram concluded that Ben-Hadad must have been picking a fight because he had no capability to heal the man. Elisha heard about the incident and sent a messenger to Naaman, not even taking the time to meet with him personally, which offended him greatly.

If you stop to think about it, his reaction makes sense; Naaman held the rank of general, had immense troops at his command, held great political favor, and military success, and felt slighted. After his own servants talked some sense into him, he washed in the Jordan River as originally instructed and experienced an amazing and permanent healing from his illness. As a result, Naaman clearly experienced a true faith in Yahweh, changing his life not only physically but spiritually.

The Point:

Even the most casual reading of the Old Testament creates the distinct impression that Israel needed to stay
culturally distinct from the nations around them. At
first glance that might seem a bit elitist or paranoid; the
simple fact of the matter was that the prohibitions were
aimed at effectively maintaining their collective faith in
Yahweh.

The various people groups inhabiting the region
practiced fertility religions that included ritual sex, child
sacrifice, idol worship, and many other pagan practices.
Even later as the Jewish people dominated the land and
exerted political influence over the geography, the possibility of diluting their religious expression was still a
danger.

When reviewing the history of the Israelite monarchy, you can see that this was not an idle concern. It
created numerous issues for the welfare of the nation
and resulted in the eventual exile of the nation. That
resulted in a deep suspicion of "outsiders" that persisted
rather heavily until the time of Jesus Himself and in
some measure has trickled into modern Christianity by
default. Often, it seems that many well-intentioned followers of Christ view the world outside church as dangerous and essentially enemy territory.

Granted, a great deal of hostility exists toward
Christianity these days in the media and society in general, but this has sometimes created a mindset that is
more about reaction and protection than anything else.
In the account described in 2 Kings, the young Israelite
girl had genuine concern for the wellbeing of someone

not only who did not share her faith but was part of a nation that at times was at war with her own. This nameless girl effectively engaged a life-altering situation with compassion as well as how her faith in Yahweh could address the problem.

As you and I let down the walls around us and engage with the world around us, we can invite Christ to make an impact through us. When we place our trust in Jesus, we become His hands and feet, and we can bring personal and spiritual transformation to places that would not otherwise have it. Certainly you and I encounter risks in doing so—risks of misunderstanding, risks of possible rejection, and risks of offense by others; truth be told though, there is *nothing* worthwhile in life that ever happens without taking chances.

> Then some Pharisees and teachers of the law came to Jesus from Jerusalem and asked, "Why do your disciples break the tradition of the elders? They don't wash their hands before they eat!" Jesus replied, "And why do you break the command of God for the sake of your tradition? For God said, 'Honor your father and mother' and 'Anyone who curses his father or mother must be put to death.' But you say that if a man says to his father or mother, 'Whatever help you might otherwise have received from me is a gift devoted to God,' he is not to 'honor his father' with it. Thus you nullify the word of God for the sake of your tradition..."Jesus called the crowd to him and said, "Listen and understand. What goes into a man's mouth does

not make him 'unclean,' but what comes out of his
mouth that is what makes him 'unclean.' "

Matthew 15:1–11 (NIV)

Background:

The Pharisees and Jesus clashed constantly. At times
the confrontations were deliberate and calculated and
designed to trap Him; on other occasions the conflicts
were more impromptu and casual, as the case is in
this passage. Jewish law, based on the Torah (Genesis
through Deuteronomy), had several distinct divisions,
namely moral (standards of conduct), civil (relating
to government operations), and ceremonial (religious
practices, observances, etc.).

In addition, some Jewish teachers believed that
prior to his death, Moses passed on spoken laws (or oral
tradition) passed on to Joshua and from father to son,
to that time. The Pharisees held that oral tradition as
equally authoritative to the written law and binding, to
which they refer in this instance, namely, washing hands
before eating.

Since our society makes a large emphasis on personal hygiene this may not sound unusual at all, but this
practice had more to do with religious symbolism than
sanitation. Cleanliness was not just next to godliness
but a part of it! Jesus made a very blunt response that
offended them doubly.

First, He pointed out that they violated the actual
written law by their supposedly binding traditions, in

this case denying necessary support of their own parents using a type of religious loophole.

Second, Jesus labeled all of the so-called oral tradition as meaningless and actually an obstacle to truly following God, effectively calling it hypocrisy. Looking at this type of exchange it is easy to see why Jesus's opponents wanted Him literally out of the way.[3]

The Point:

Because of the nature of cultural and personal values, we can easily forget how many of our opinions and personal habits came from fallible sources as opposed to those that are actually biblically based. Observance of the LORD's Supper or Communion illustrates this well. In most evangelical traditions, the bread and juice are placed in small cups and trays, draped over with a white cloth, and everyone celebrates the ceremony together, often served by deacons, elders, or church staff members.

The writings of the New Testament speak about this ritual and how to observe it, but leave a number of details out. The small cups and trays are very practical but invented by a rural Baptist pastor, and the use of juice rather than wine began with Mr. Welch.[4]

In addition, the white drape often used served the purpose of simply keeping flies off the juice and bread. Nothing is wrong with any of these newer contributions, but understanding their human origin is important as well. Otherwise, items based on simple tradition or personal preferences become elevated to the point of equal to the Bible itself.

Some Christians believe strongly in political action, while others try to avoid it. Certain churches feel that celebrating Halloween amounts to practicing witchcraft, while others see it as a benign cultural event (dentists may have objections to the sugar content but that is hardly theological).

Another rather infamous bone of contention centers on the recreational use of alcohol, with entire denominations mandating abstinence and other groups pronouncing it just fine in moderation. Taking questionable arguments and making them somehow essential to the very nature of true faith borders on the same error that the opponents of Jesus made.

> Dear friends, I urge you, as aliens and strangers in the world, to abstain from sinful desires, which war against your soul. Live such good lives among the pagans that, though they accuse you of doing wrong, they may see your good deeds and glorify God on the day he visits us. Submit yourselves for the LORD's sake to every authority instituted among men: whether to the king, as the supreme authority, or to governors, who are sent by him to punish those who do wrong and to commend those who do right. For it is God's will that by doing good you should silence the ignorant talk of foolish men. Live as free men, but do not use your freedom as a cover-up for evil; live as servants of God. Show proper respect to everyone: Love the brotherhood of believers, fear God, honor the king.

> 1 Peter 2:9–17 (NIV)

Background:

Peter had walked with Jesus firsthand, personally witnessed His teachings, miracles, and way of life, as well as serving as a prominent leader in the early Christian church. In the first book that bears his name, Peter addresses believers living throughout Asia Minor, or modern-day Turkey; at the time of writing, these followers of Jesus had begun to experience mistreatment and persecution. Part of the purpose of the book is to give encouragement to a group under various pressures regarding their faith.

In this particular section, Peter addresses the responsibilities of Christians toward those around them, including the state, specifically the Roman government in this case. In addition, these believers are urged to follow the laws of the land, show high regard to fellow believers, and act in a respectable manner toward everyone. What is striking in verse 17 is the words, "Show proper respect to everyone."

In the context of the increasingly hostile stance of Rome toward Christianity, this has immense significance; the words do not read "Show respect to the deserving" or "Show respect to those who act respectably"—it plainly says *everyone*. Peter's instructions to believers in Christ, then, emphasize civility, respect, and even kindness toward all, demonstrating the love and character of Christ.[5]

The Point:

God created the human race with freedom of choice and individuality "standard from the factory" so to speak. As mentioned previously, this makes it virtually impossible for complete and total agreement on personal viewpoints. Naturally, we have strong feelings about certain beliefs, standards, and opinions above others and stand ready to defend them; nothing is wrong with having strong feelings.

Often, however, our interactions with those holding opposing points of view can generate more heat (conflict) than light (understanding). The more emotion and/or passion surrounding beliefs or positions, the greater the possibility we have for taking the matter somehow personally and reacting in a less than rational manner—it may not flatter, but it does reflect common human experience.

Over the years I have personally witnessed many a Christian (across all denominations and backgrounds) act in remarkably rude, disrespectful, and downright ugly ways toward others simply because they did not agree with them. Renowned speaker and author Chuck Swindoll put it this way:

> People who seek control don't see the world in conformity with either truth or untruth, but in terms of agreement with them ... and one thing that is always true of controllers; what they cannot control, they destroy.[6]

We gain nothing through rudeness, mistreatment and disrespect toward others; in fact we compromise the mission of Christ in the world around us. You and I represent Jesus on the planet as ambassadors and living proof that faith makes a positive difference, and too many people have made the opposite impression. A common phrase I have said to those outside Christian circles is: "God is easier to please than some of His children." Let me reemphasize that this never requires surrendering our beliefs, opinions, or even truth. I am not advocating eliminating or watering down revealed truth in any way. What we need to do, however, is to treat others with genuine respect instead of running them over.

> Now the tax collectors and "sinners" were all gathering around to hear him. But the Pharisees and the teachers of the law muttered, "This man welcomes sinners and eats with them."… Jesus continued: "There was a man who had two sons. The younger one said to his father, 'Father, give me my share of the estate.' So he divided his property between them. "Not long after that, the younger son got together all he had, set off for a distant country and there squandered his wealth in wild living. After he had spent everything, there was a severe famine in that whole country, and he began to be in need. So he went and hired himself out to a citizen of that country, who sent him to his fields to feed pigs… When he came to his senses, he said, 'How many of my father's hired men have food to spare, and here I am starving to death!' So he got up and went

to his father. But while he was still a long way off, his father saw him and was filled with compassion for him; he ran to his son, threw his arms around him and kissed him. "The son said to him, 'Father, I have sinned against heaven and against you. I am no longer worthy to be called your son.' "But the father said to his servants, 'Quick! Bring the best robe and put it on him. Put a ring on his finger and sandals on his feet. Bring the fattened calf and kill it. Let's have a feast and celebrate. For this son of mine was dead and is alive again; he was lost and is found.' So they began to celebrate. "Meanwhile, the older son was in the field. When he came near the house, he heard music and dancing. So he called one of the servants and asked him what was going on. 'Your brother has come,' he replied, 'and your father has killed the fattened calf because he has him back safe and sound.' "The older brother became angry and refused to go in. So his father went out and pleaded with him. But he answered his father, 'Look! All these years I've been slaving for you and never disobeyed your orders. Yet you never gave me even a young goat so I could celebrate with my friends. But when this son of yours who has squandered your property with prostitutes comes home, you kill the fattened calf for him!' 'My son,' the father said, 'you are always with me, and everything I have is yours. But we had to celebrate and be glad, because this brother of yours was dead and is alive again; he was lost and is found.' "

Luke 15:1–2, 11–32 (NIV)

Background:

One of the best-known stories from the life of Jesus is entitled "the Prodigal Son," and the context is critical to understand. Luke, the account of the life of Jesus aimed at the Gentile population, is probably the most chronological of all the gospels. One of the prominent Jewish religious groups of Jesus's day was the Pharisees, who were well trained and highly structured in the observance of their faith.

As they observed the religious and social outcasts gathering around Him they took serious issue with it and even made disparaging comments about it. One of the things to understand in near-eastern culture was that eating with someone implied friendship and acceptance (Wight, 1983).

In response to the grumblings of the Pharisees, Jesus told the parable about a family with two male heirs, the youngest of which demanded his share of the estate, left home, and went to live in a Gentile land some distance away. This young man then proceeded to live a life of wild partying that rapidly depleted his newfound wealth, and when the money was gone, so were all of his so-called friends. Coincidentally, a famine fell on the region, reflecting dire economic conditions that affected everyone, making his situation move from merely difficult to exceedingly desperate.

Since the context assumed that the young man was Jewish, the fact that he took any sort of job feeding pigs paints the picture of someone who had hit absolute bottom. The food fed to the pigs (carob pods) depicts emergency rations and adds even more desperation to his situation. As with most stubborn people, only at this point did the young man realize how bad things were and how well off his situation had been at home. Even the most menial day laborer on his father's property had ample provisions, and here he was starving in a terrible place.

He traveled home, confessed his unworthiness to have even the lowest place in the family, and asked for forgiveness; his father gladly received his lost son back and hosted a party so lavish that Donald Trump would have been envious! The older son heard the loud merrymaking, and, after hearing it was celebrating his wayward brother's return, refused to have any part of it.

As the father spoke to him, the older son took issue more with his father's generosity and forgiveness than even his brother's bad behaviors—"But when *this son of yours* who has squandered your property with prostitutes comes home, you kill the fattened calf for him!"

Note that the older son did not even acknowledge his brother's relationship but was angry over his own father's actions of restoring him as a son. Jesus essentially identified the character of the older son as the self-righteous Pharisees—who essentially took God to task for not elevating them to greatness and instead accepting worthless people into forgiveness and relationship with Himself.[7]

The Point:

As human beings, we possess curiously short spans of memory, and often, remarkably selective memory. When we recall past events, certain aspects get conveniently omitted, altered, or retold in ways that either give us less embarrassment or greater praise; every man or woman is the hero of their own story, that is simply human nature. Many times we forget, however, how we got to where we are, so to speak. A personally and morally successful life does not simply materialize out of thin air with the wave of a magic wand; it requires commitment, wise and consistent decision-making, and actions that lead to positive consequences.

That same type of situation can exist for those who have possessed and practiced an effective faith for a long period of time; one can end up forgetting the initial struggles, the mistakes, the really, *really* bad decisions, and other circumstances that eventually brought them to a stable place.

None of us by virtue of our imperfect and finite human natures can ever claim to be superior to someone else, as we all have the equal capability of royally screwing things up. Keep in mind that the Bible records many of these mistakes in vivid detail—Abraham claiming that his wife Sarah was actually his sister, Joseph's brothers selling him into slavery, Moses murdering an Egyptian guard, David committing adultery and killing a man to cover it up, just to name a few. Even upon close examination, all of us have gruesome aspects to our lives and personalities that could easily show up if scrutinized enough.

All of us fail, all of us do not live up to what we know we should do, all of us make stupid choices, all of us ultimately need the power and presence of Jesus Christ to keep our lives in balance. The phrase "but for the grace of God, there go I" has deep meaning in this context; the second that we think we are somehow better or morally superior to someone else, the more we resemble the self-righteous religious bigots than the Christ that we serve. When Jesus truly lives in our hearts, His life is lived out through us, at times in spite of us, but always out toward others.

Questions

1. What have you done this past week that clearly demonstrates that you love God with:

   - All your heart? How have you expressed your feelings to the person of Christ tangibly? How do you enjoy expressing yourself to Him?

   - All your mind? How do you engage your mind in thoughts and understanding more of God's truth? Do you ever journal the things that come to mind?

   - All your strength? How do you match your greatest passions in life with your faith in Jesus Christ? What ways do you seek to truly give back to Him?

2. How can you show the love of God toward others in some concrete way? Have you asked Christ to use you, your talents, resources, and time to make an actual difference in the lives of specific people? What can you do differently just this week to dem-

onstrate God's love to someone in your circle of influence?

3. On a scale of one (lowest) to five (highest), please rank how confident you feel in how you handle the following areas of your life:

- Home and family
- Work and career
- Personal friendships
- Faith/church
- Finances
- Planning

4. Of the areas you scored lowest, how open are you to advice from others? How often do you put it into practice?

5. Of the areas you scored highest, how often do you ignore advice from others? How can the area of your greatest strength become one of weakness? How does pride play into that?

Prayer

LORD, teach me how to listen instead of speak; to observe instead of act; to understand instead of assume; to love instead of judge. Help me to view myself as valuable in Your sight but capable of mistakes in how I see people, how I act toward people, and how I choose to live. Help me to remember what things were like before

You came into my life and the enormous difference You still make in me every day. Allow my words to be those You would say to those I encounter; allow me to see things as they truly are, including myself, and give me humility in every situation.

Do not allow me to judge others but to reveal Your life within me in a way that brings warmth, healing, and truth in a relevant manner. Help me to continue growing in my life, my faith, and in all of my relationships. Allow me the honor of being as magnetic to people in my places of influence as You were in Yours. Give me the courage to stand for truth, but the grace to live it in a way that honors You and those You created in Your image. In Jesus's name, Amen.

End Notes

Chapter 1

[1]   David Kinnaman, UnChristian: What a New Generation Thinks About Christianity (Grand Rapids: Baker Books, 2007), p. 91.

[2]   Leon Wood, *A Survey of Israel's History* (Grand Rapids: Zondervan Publishing, 1970), p. 207.

[3]   D. Edmond Hiebert, *The Epistle of James* (Chicago: Moody Press, 1977), pp. 145–154.

[4]   J. Dwight Pentecost, *The Words and Works of Jesus Christ* (Grand Rapids: Zondervan Publishing, 1981), pp. 307–313.

Chapter 2

[1]   Joseph Pickett, ed., *The American Heritage Dictionary of the English Language* (Boston:Houghton Mifflin Co., 2006), p 201.

2 Millard Erickson, *Christian Theology* (Grand Rapids: Baker Book House, 1998), pp. 495–517.

3 Lewis Sperry Chafer, *Systematic Theology: Angelology, Anthropology, and Hamartiology* (Dallas: Dallas Seminary Press, 1947), pp. 161–170.

4 Millard Erickson, *Christian Theology* (Grand Rapids: Baker Book House, 1998), pp. 516.

5 Mark Young, *The Guinness Book of World Records* 1999 (New York: Bantam Books, 1999), p. 102.

6 Millard Erickson, *Christian Theology* (Grand Rapids: Baker Book House, 1998), pp. 491.

7 D. Edmond Hiebert, *An Introduction to the New Testament: The Pauline Epistles* (Chicago: Moody Press, 1977), pp. 106–116.

8 Leon Wood, *A Survey of Israel's History* (Grand Rapids: Zondervan Publishing, 1970), pp. 235–236.

Chapter 3

1 Craig Blomberg, *The New American Commentary: Matthew* (Nashville: Broadman Press, 1992), pp. 334–336.

2 Leon Wood, *A Survey of Israel's History* (Grand Rapids: Zondervan Publishing, 1970), p. 69–72.

3   J. Dwight Pentecost, *The Words and Works of Jesus Christ* (Grand Rapids: Zondervan Publishing, 1981), pp. 473–477.

Chapter 4

1   Joseph Pickett, ed., *The American Heritage Dictionary of the English Language* (Boston: Houghton Mifflin Co., 2006), pp.

2   J. Dwight Pentecost, *The Words and Works of Jesus Christ* (Grand Rapids: Zondervan Publishing, 1981), pp. 537–560.

3   Felix Just, Ph. D., Ethnic/National/Religious Groups in Biblical Times (http://catholic-resources.org/Bible/Ethnic_Groups.htm.)

4   *Ibid.*

5   Merrill Tenney, *John: The Gospel of Belief* (Grand Rapids: Eerdmans Publishing Company, 1976), p. 91–95.

6   John Polhill, *The New American Commentary: Acts* (Nashville: Broadman Press, 1992), p. 323–334.

7   *Ibid*, pp. 365–378.

Chapter 5

1   J. Dwight Pentecost, *The Words and Works of Jesus Christ* (Grand Rapids: Zondervan Publishing, 1981), pp. 282–283.

2 Matthew Henry, *Matthew Henry's Commentary on the Whole Bible* (Nashville: Thomas Nelson Publishers, 2008), p. 1110.

3 Leon Wood, *A Survey of Israel's History* (Grand Rapids: Zondervan Publishing, 1970), pp. 173–175.

4 Iris Leos Hickenbottom, *Prostitution: Then and Now* (*http://www.cwrl.utexas.edu/~ulrich/femhist/sex_work.shtml#Modernviews*)

5 Jack Graham, *Daily Word* (*http://www.christianity.com/devotionals/powerpoint/11608399/*).

6 D. Edmond Hiebert, *An Introduction to the New Testament: The Pauline Epistles* (Chicago: Moody Press, 1977), pp. 71–81.

7 Leslie Allen, *The Books of Joel, Obadiah, Jonah and Micah* (Grand Rapids: Eerdmans Publishing Company, 1976), pp. 244–259.

Chapter 6

1 Elisabeth Kubler-Ross, *On Death and Dying* (New York: Scribner, 1969).

2 *The Matrix*. DVD. Directed by Larry and Andy Wachowski (Burbank, CA: Warner Brothers, 1999).

3 *Diary of A Mad Black Woman*. DVD. Directed by Tyler Perry (Vancouver, BC: Lionsgate Entertainment, 2005).

4 Leon Wood, *A Survey of Israel's History* (Grand Rapids: Zondervan Publishing,   1970), pp. 277–278.

5 J. Dwight Pentecost, *The Words and Works of Jesus Christ* (Grand Rapids: Zondervan Publishing, 1981), pp. 267–270.

6 Merrill Tenney, *John: The Gospel of Belief* (Grand Rapids: Eerdmans Publishing Company, 1976), pp. 104–106.

Chapter 7

1 Robert Stein, *The New American Commentary: Luke* (Nashville: Broadman Press, 1992), p. 465–470.

2 Russell Dilday, *The Communicator's Commentary: I & II Kings* (Waco: Word Press, 1987), pp. 302–308.

3 Craig Blomberg, *The New American Commentary: Matthew* (Nashville: Broadman Press, 1992), pp. 237–240.

4 Paige Patterson, ed., *Baptist Theology: Questions & Answers*, http://www.baptisttheology.org/questions.cfm

[5] D. Edmond Hiebert, *An Introduction to the New Testament: The Non-Pauline Epistles and Revelation* (Chicago: Moody Press, 1977), pp. 113–124.

[6] Charles Swindoll, *Walk with Jesus* (Nashville: Thomas Nelson Publishers, 2009), p.16.

[7] John MacArthur, *A Tale of Two Sons: Study Guide* (Nashville: Thomas Nelson Publishers, 2008), pp. 75–83.

Bibliography

Allen, Leslie. The Books of Joel, Obadiah, Jonah
    and Micah. Grand Rapids: Eerdmans
    Publishing Company, 1976.

Blomberg, Craig. The New American Commentary:
    Matthew. Nashville: Broadman Press, 1992.

Chafer, Lewis Sperry. Systematic Theology:
    Angelology, Anthropology, and
    Hamartiology. Dallas: Dallas Seminary Press,
    1947.

Diary of A Mad Black Woman. DVD. Directed
    by Tyler Perry. Vancouver, BC: Lionsgate
    Entertainment, 2005.

Dilday, Russell. The Communicator's Commentary:
    I & II Kings. Waco: Word Press, 1987.

Erickson, Millard. Christian Theology. Grand
    Rapids: Baker Book House, 1998.

Graham, Jack. Daily Word. http://www.christian-ity.com/devotionals/powerpoint/11608399/.

Henry, Matthew. Matthew Henry's Commentary on the Whole Bible. Nashville: Thomas Nelson Publishers, 2008.

Hickenbottom, Iris Leos. Prostitution: Then and Now. http://www.cwrl.utexas.edu/~ulrich/femhist/sex_work.shtml#Modernviews

Hiebert, D. Edmond. The Epistle of James. Chicago: Moody Press, 1977.

Hiebert, D. Edmond. An Introduction to the New Testament: The Non-Pauline Epistles and Revelation. Chicago: Moody Press, 1977.

Hiebert, D. Edmond. An Introduction to the New Testament: The Pauline Epistles.

Chicago: Moody Press, 1977. Just, Felix, Ph. D. Ethnic/National/Religious Groups in Biblical Times. http://catholic-resources.org/Bible/Ethnic_Groups.htm.

Kinnaman, David. UnChristian: What a New Generation Thinks About Christianity. Grand Rapids: Baker Books, 2007.

Kubler-Ross, Elisabeth. On Death and Dying. New York: Scribner, 1969.

MacArthur, John. A Tale of Two Sons: Study Guide, Nashville: Thomas Nelson Publishers, 2008

Melick, Richard. The New American Commentary: Philippians, Colossians & Philemon. Nashville: Broadman Press, 1991.

Patterson, Paige, ed. Baptist Theology: Questions & Answers, http://www.baptisttheology.org/questions.cfm

Pentecost, J. Dwight. The Words and Works of Jesus Christ. Grand Rapids: Zondervan Publishing, 1981.

Pickett, Joseph, ed., The American Heritage Dictionary of the English Language, Boston:

Houghton Mifflin Co., 2006.

Polhill, John. The New American Commentary: Acts. Nashville: Broadman Press, 1992.

Simon, Urie. Joseph and His Brothers: A Story of Change. http://www.lookstein.org/library.php

Stein, Robert. The New American Commentary: Luke. Nashville: Broadman Press, 1992

Swindoll, Charles . Walk with Jesus. Nashville: Thomas Nelson Publishers, 2009

Tenney, Merrill. John: The Gospel of Belief. Grand
　　　　Rapids: Eerdmans Publishing Company,
　　　　1976.

The Matrix. DVD. Directed by Larry and Andy
　　　　Wachowski. Burbank, CA: Warner
　　　　Brothers, 1999.

Wood, Leon. A Survey of Israel's History. Grand
　　　　Rapids: Zondervan Publishing, 1970.

Wood, Leon. The Prophets of Israel. Grand
　　　　Rapids: Baker Book House, 1979.

Wight, Fred. Maners and Customs of Bible Lands.
　　　　Chicago: Moody Press, 1983

Young, Mark. The Guinness Book of World
　　　　Records 1999. New York: Bantam Books,
　　　　1999.